If It Doesn't Work,

Read the Instructions

If It Doesn't

Read

Work, the Instructions

CHARLES KLAMKIN

STEIN AND DAY/*Publishers*/New York

Contents

1

Thank You, Betty Furness

Is THERE REALLY any way the average consumer can walk into a store and purchase a major appliance and be confident that:

1. The item was best suited to his needs?
2. The purchase price was the lowest available?
3. The financing charges were not exorbitant?
4. The product will deliver the performance claimed?
5. Service, if needed, will be prompt and efficient?
6. The warranty affords real protection of his investment?

A major appliance such as a refrigerator, freezer, washer, dryer, stove, television set, or stereo set represents for most families one of their largest capital investments. Most likely one or more of these items will have to be bought or replaced at least once a year. Yet in spite of the relatively high expense involved in these purchases, very few people know more than is needed to buy a box of corn flakes or a bar of soap.

The appliance business is a jungle where the pitfalls are shoddy design and construction, cloudy warranty claims, poor or nonexistent service, lack of a firm price, and costly financing arrangements. Manufacturers load a product with costly extra trimmings and features that add little to its usefulness or durability but a great deal to its cost. An awareness of the "come-on," the high-pressure sales techniques, and the overblown claims for performance and service will help the shopper to make a sound buying decision. Knowing how to find a reliable dealer, what questions to ask, and what basic features to look for in a product will save the buyer a lot of money and avoid a great deal of future aggravation.

Because the appliance industry has been delivering ever more complicated equipment for household use, production has far outstripped the supply of manpower and facilities needed to keep these sophisticated products in good repair. The public's indignation and frustration concerning bad manufacture and poor service has finally found government agencies willing to take a sympathetic attitude toward the problem.

The Johnson administration reacted to the demand for more energetic federal action by appointing actress Betty Furness as Special Assistant to the President for Consumer Affairs. The political advantages of creating a bureau to protect the consumer's interests were not overlooked by Mayor Lindsay of New York. He topped the federal government in the glamour-image race by appointing Bess Myerson Grant, a former Miss America, to head the city's Department of Consumer Affairs.

Very little in the nature of concrete reform or corrective legislation has yet evolved from the efforts of Miss Furness or her successor, Mrs. Virginia Knauer. At this point their major contribution has been to bring the situation to the attention of the public, Congress, and the industry. The popularity of their cause has stirred congressmen to call for committee investigations, new laws to strengthen product warranties, and assurances that they will be fulfilled. The threat of government action has sent the appliance industry scurrying to clean its house. The industry sees the government taking measures similar to those imposed on the automobile industry to correct many of the same abuses.

To dramatize how little knowledge the consumer brings to the purchase of a major appliance such as a refrigerator, compare what takes place when one goes to buy a new car. First, every car buyer usually has a pretty strong bias for or against a particular make. From his experience of having to replace his automobile much more frequently than home appliances, the buyer has learned what makes of cars have performed better for him and lasted longer. He knows from the new car sticker exactly what the price of the car and various options and accessories will be. He can determine whether the additional performance, luxury, or enhanced appearance is worth the additional investment. If the car buyer is interested in economical operation, he selects a car with a smaller engine, popular-size tires, standard transmission, and as few power-consuming options as possible.

The warranty on a new car, although it has come in recently for its share of criticism, does have value. It states that for a specified period of time or number of miles, mechanical defects will be corrected at the factory's expense. The car buyer can usually see the workshop adjacent to the showroom. The sight of uniformed mechanics, hydraulic lifts, specialized repair equipment, and a parts department convinces the buyer that the dealer has the means to handle a problem if it arises.

When it comes to buying a refrigerator or other expensive appliance, the buyer has very little expertise or experience to help him. For someone setting up a new household, it is his first time in the market. Otherwise, the purchase is made under pressure because the old appliance has collapsed or is about to collapse. The chances are very good that if the old appliance or television set is more than ten or fifteen years old the company that made it has either sold out, given up its manufacture, or gone out of business. If you had good results with a Crossley, Bendix, Dexter, Thor, Universal, Majestic, FADA, International Harvester, or Stromberg Carlson, forget it—they don't make them any more.

If you are concerned about the monthly operating cost of a new refrigerator, don't expect the salesman to tell you that his flashy frost-free model will cost more than twice as much to operate as your old one. The television commercials show a harried housewife hacking the glacier off an old clunker of a refrigerator. The same commercial should, but doesn't, point out that they make a perfectly reliable, amply-sized model that sells for considerably less than the flashy frost-free, ice-making model that solves all the lady's problems. Nor is it pointed out that a less elaborate refrigerator that needs defrosting only two or three times a year would cost only half as much to operate and has a considerably lower selling price.

It is natural for any industry to ignore the negative aspects of its products, but industry does have a responsibility to make its market aware that added conveniences and capacity, like additional horsepower and power options on autos, just cost more to run.

One of the first things a retail appliance salesman is taught is to "qualify the customer." He is told to find out how many members there are in the customer's family, how often the family shops for food, and whether it uses a great deal of frozen food or entertains extensively. This is so that the salesman does not waste time trying to sell the lady who lives alone next to the supermarket the largest refrigerator in the store. Otherwise the name of the game is to get the biggest, fanciest, most jazzed-up box possible into the customer's home.

When the subject of service is raised by an appliance customer, the assurance is usually verbal. Rarely is an appliance or electronic repair shop visible from a retail sales floor. The customer is told that the dealer has a repair shop equipped like MIT and staffed by Ph.D.'s from all the factory training schools. Or, if he lives in a major metropolitan market, the customer is told how fortunate he is. If he should need service he will be taken care of by a factory-operated central service depot. These service agencies, owned by the manufacturers, perform this function for all the dealers in their market selling their particular brand.

It is the salesman's job to weave a spell that convinces the customer that he is getting the best product made at the lowest price in the history of the store and that the service man will ring his doorbell before he hangs up the phone.

The spell is broken when the appliance arrives inoperative or conks out later and repeated calls for service get shuffled or ignored. It is broken when, particularly in the case of minority groups, the buyers find that they have been outrageously overcharged or loaded with unconscionable finance charges.

These are the abuses that have brought about the recent consumer revolt. The rise of "consumerism" has given new importance to agencies such as Better Business Bureaus on the local level, Offices for Consumer Protection on the state level, and the Federal Trade Commission in Washington, D.C. These agencies, especially those that operate with public funds, are particularly sensitive to this movement, and their activities have greater impact because of much wider coverage by the press.

Paul Dixon, former Federal Trade Commissioner chairman, threatened in a speech before a convention of manufacturers of electronic goods that if these companies do not fulfill their obligations to the consumer, the government will seek legislation to enforce these warranties. Also vocal in this area are spokesmen for those minorities whose members have consistently been the victims of the most flagrant and unethical retail practices.

The purpose of this book is to help the consumer become a more sophisticated, less gullible buyer. When the time comes to make a purchase of a major appliance the informed buyer will want to know:

1. The reputation and quality of the dealer.
2. If the item is best suited to his purpose.
3. Exactly what service he is entitled to, who is going to do it, and how competent they are.
4. What redress he has if dissatisfied.
5. That the price paid is as low as can be obtained commensurate with adequate service guarantees.
6. That the finance charges are as low as any available.
7. That the appliance purchased was what he really wanted and not what the store desired to move.

⊙

2

Back to the
Drawing Board

IN THEIR RUSH to produce and market the millions of home appliances sold each year, the manufacturers have been guilty of a great number of engineering and design errors. These mistakes have caused the products either to perform badly or not at all or to break down soon after delivery. In addition to these major blunders, there are innumerable instances of minor design or construction lapses that are as annoying as they are inexcusable.

The results of this shoddy planning and fabricating have cost the manufacturers a lot of money. Dealers have had to struggle to correct the problems and placate their customers, who are the real victims. The consumer has been the ultimate guinea pig of untried products and unproven refinements in technology and design. Appliances and television sets have been delivered to the public that were incapable of performing the function that they were bought for, or have required an inordinate amount of costly service, or were downright unsafe.

It would seem inconceivable that Kelvinator, a company which had been making refrigeration for fifty years, would bring out an expensive model which failed to maintain the proper food-keeping temperature in its fresh-food compartment. It also seems difficult to believe that RCA, the largest manufacturer of television sets, would deliver a complete line of television sets which would fail to perform except in strong-signal metropolitan areas. In the so-called fringe areas, where at least 50 percent of the sets are sold, these television sets were helpless. So were the dealers who sold them.

A number of years ago, the Hotpoint division of General Electric brought out an automatic washer incorporating a new type of transmission. These washers gave so much trouble that for several years afterward Hotpoint permitted their owners to exchange them for new models upon payment of a ninety-dollar fee. This was a rare instance of a manufacturer actually taking back a faulty appliance even though the buyers had been put to a great deal of extra expense and aggravation.

There have been plenty of these major goofs, but there are also minor ones which are continuous headaches to dealers, servicemen, and owners. In this category have been the screens on early black-and-white television sets which would become fogged over between the picture tube and safety glass and couldn't be cleaned unless the complete chassis was removed from the rear of the set. Usually this was a job for a serviceman; it became unnecessary when someone in product planning woke up and attached a face plate to the outside of the cabinet with a few easily removed screws.

The Kelvinator Division of American Motors, which was recently sold to White Consolidated Industries, was a pioneer in the production of "duplex" style refrigerators. In this type of refrigerator, which Kelvinator first sold in 1957 as the "Fooderama," the refrigerator and freezer sections are side by side with separate full-length doors. This was a departure from the single door refrigerator or the two door box with the freezer compartment either above or below the food compartment. Because not too many houses or apartments could accommodate the Fooderama's bulk or 41-inch width, it sold only moderately well.

However, the Admiral Corporation, which had been a relatively minor factor in the refrigerator business for about thirty years, adopted the duplex concept, streamlined it, and manufactured a more compact model which was only 36 inches wide. This more realistically sized refrigerator was enormously successful and ultimately led to the introduction of a complete line of duplexes by Admiral and other manufacturers in widths of 30, 32, 33, 36, 42, and 48 inches. The race of the manufacturers of refrigerators to cash in on this lucrative market caused them to design, tool, and produce these complicated refrigeration systems without adequate time for design study, component quality control, or field testing.

Admiral and Hotpoint had trouble with their boxes maintaining even temperatures throughout the large food compartments. Food near the upper refrigerating coils would sometimes freeze, while the temperatures below would be too warm to keep food safely. Many makers of the large two-zoned boxes had an inordinate number of compressor failures. These large refrigerators were rushed into production with compressor units which were either undersized or only marginally efficient for the job they had to do. On very hot days, one after another, the inadequate compressors ceased working.

When Kelvinator decided to make the compact duplex refrigerators, it entered the market in 1966 with a 36-inch Fooderama. It was a well-styled refrigerator, competitively priced, and initial sales were good. However, Kelvinator, the originator of the "side-by-side" refrigerator, with more experience than anyone else in the industry, pulled a boner. The food compartment, in most cases, would not run cold enough and complaints poured in from customers and dealers all over the country.

Engineers at Kelvinator had to find the cause and cure it quickly, and they finally published a service bulletin which described the steps necessary to correct this condition. This was a four-page memorandum which told the servicemen how to rework certain tubing, drill new holes, and make other mechanical changes, and called for the addition of a repair kit to make the refrigerator work. Servicemen and dealers were given a $17.50 labor allowance to make these modifications. That amount did not begin to cover the dealer's aggravation and expense in sending trained men to take apart and remanufacture a new five-hundred-dollar refrigerator in a customer's home. This type of failure points up the lack of proper quality control and inadequate field testing in the appliance industry.

Although the move to frost-free or total nondefrosting type of refrigerator was introduced about ten years ago, it is only within the last five years that this system has outsold the conventional type of box. In the frost-free system a fan is employed to circulate the air in the freezer section. The moisture in this air is condensed in the rear of the space. Periodically, this coil and the coils controlling the food compartment are defrosted automatically.

In all this time, the system, whether called frostless, frost-free, or no-frost, has still not been debugged. Typical failures have been fan motors, fan-motor switches, which are imbedded in the wall of the box and are actuated when the door is opened or closed, and defrost timer controls. Westinghouse made a defrost timer that counted the number of times the refrigerator door was opened, but it was abandoned in 1962 when it was found that nearly every timer had to be replaced within the first year or two of operation.

On a smaller scale, but just as irksome to everyone, was Admiral's problem in 1965 with plastic shelf supports on refrigerators and freezers. Fixed shelves in the food compartment were supported by small plastic knobs which developed the habit of shearing off when any weight was placed on the shelf. Food and liquids tumbled all over the inside of the refrigerator, making an unholy mess for the housewife. Admiral eventually recognized that the problem was epidemic and sent out a service bulletin suggesting the replacement of the support with one of an improved material. Yet this ten-cent part caused a big public-relations problem for the factory and the dealers. Also, a serviceman was required to replace it.

At about the same time Hotpoint ran into a similar problem with the plastic anchors that fasten the shelves to the door liners on refrigerators and freezers. These would break off when the door was opened and dump the contents of the shelves all over the floor.

For a short time Westinghouse thought that it would relieve the housewife of the onerous task of yanking on a door handle in order to open the refrigerator door. It came out with an electrically operated latch which merely had to be touched in order to release the door. This was fine until there was a power failure or the mechanism malfunctioned. Then the refrigerator became a vault in which the food was as inaccessible as if it had been stored at a bank.

This problem was dramatized when a community of Hasidic Jews in Brooklyn purchased about twenty of these refrigerators. This super-Orthodox sect would not permit any mechanical apparatus to function on the Sabbath and every Friday before sundown they would unplug their Westinghouse refrigerators. Now this meant that they would starve. Since they were prohibited from doing any physical labor or carrying money on the Sabbath, they could not wrestle the door open or go out and buy more food. When their predicament was relayed to Westinghouse the New York branch manager was instructed not to argue, but just to exchange the boxes for some with conventional latches.

Early in 1966, owners of new Magic Chef gas ranges discovered that the porcelain enamel finish inside their ovens was flaking off. Upon investigation, Magic Chef found the cause to be improper annealing of the steel furnished to them by their supplier. In a move untypical of the industry as a whole, Magic Chef promptly shipped replacement liners wherever they were needed and gave their dealers a generous cash allowance to cover the expense of changing them.

The Philco Corporation astonished the industry by introducing a refrigerator in 1955 on which the door could be opened from either the right- or left-hand side. The idea was fine. Dealers and distributors didn't have to stock both the right- and left-hand boxes, and if the owner moved and found that the opposite door opening was more convenient he didn't have to invest in a new refrigerator. However, the doors sometimes fell off and Philco, facing the possibility of law suits for broken toes, quietly dropped the model from the line. This was another example of a product not adequately tested before distribution.

Perhaps no new product created more problems for

everyone involved than the combination automatic washer and dryer. In this appliance, clothes are washed, then dried, in the same unit. The combination saved space and saved the bother of waiting until the clothes were washed, removing and placing them in a separate machine, and resetting the timer. Philco-Bendix was the first to market the "combos," and after the usual bugs found in any new type of appliance were ironed out, it was fairly dependable and was selling well until Philco went out of the washer business.

The other laundry-equipment makers quickly rushed into production with their "combos"—and the results were almost uniformly disastrous. Westinghouse, Easy, Whirlpool, Kenmore, Maytag, General Electric, and others were plagued by so many service problems that the appliance got a bad reputation among consumers and service people; no one could be found to buy them, and dealers were afraid to sell them. Only General Electric and Sears are still distributing a few combination washer-dryers. The other manufacturers have given up on a potentially useful and profitable appliance because they did not properly engineer and test their prototype machines.

In the rapidly changing technology of the electronics industry there are countless instances where circuitry changes had to be made in the field on television sets after they had been shipped from the factory. Every television set maker is continually bombarding the dealers and servicemen with literature recommending modifications and corrective measures for the sets already in the dealers' stocks or the customers' homes.

A particularly cynical example of electronics manufacturers' rushing to market with products incorporating new techniques and design was the change to copper-etched or so-called printed circuits. In this type of television set or radio fabrication, a thin fiber board with copper-plated connections between components took the place of a "conventional" metal chassis with hand soldered wires connecting all the parts. The labor and material savings are obvious. With printed-circuit techniques, the resistors, condensers, large and small transformers, tube sockets, as well as transistors are all plugged into the board; the board is then dipped into a bath of solder. In this manner, all the parts are hooked up in one operation. Less skill is needed by the operators on the assembly line, and production is faster and cheaper.

All but a handful of electronics manufacturers brought out television sets, radios, and other products with printed circuits in the late 1950's. Technically, these sets were just as efficient as hand-wired makes, but apparently the manufacturers had not prepared for the problems that arose. The boards were fragile and quite often just the transportation from the factory to the dealer caused them to crack. Heat generated by the tubes made the boards brittle and caused expansion and contraction, which made the operation of certain circuits intermittent.

The biggest headache for the industry, however, was that they had not prepared or trained the service people to cope with the problems created by printed circuitry. All but the most skilled and conscientious servicemen threw up their hands and either refused to work on these sets or were so inept as to make matters worse.

It is more than likely that radios that suddenly stop playing or television sets that abruptly lose their picture and then mysteriously start again are displaying the symptoms of cracked or warped circuit boards. This type of complaint is very difficult and time-consuming for a serviceman to pinpoint and correct. The charges for finding and repairing this kind of trouble are sometimes more than a small table radio is worth. Formerly, a customer could take an inexpensive table radio into a store, get the tubes tested, replace a defective one, and keep the set playing for years. Now it is rare for anyone faced with an out-of-warranty repair of a transistor radio to go to the expense of getting it fixed. It is cheaper to throw it away and buy a new one.

Even the manufacturers are recognizing this disposable aspect of their products. Most of the manufacturers of imported small radios have offered replacement of defective units within the warranty period for either a minimal fee or no fee at all. Now domestic suppliers like RCA and General Electric are offering similar no-charge replacement guarantees on radios that fail within the usual ninety-day warranty period. They, too, are apparently finding that it is cheaper to replace their own products than it is to repair them. Ninety days is not too long a time for a consumer to have an umbrella over his investment. After that period is over he owns a product that everyone now concedes is just not worth fixing.

The public was not long in catching on to the strong bias of service technicians against printed circuits. The black eye given them ten years ago by servicemen is still being felt at the retail level. Of the major television producers, only Zenith was astute enough to cash in on the service preference for hand-wired circuitry. By adhering to what might be considered old-fashioned fabrication methods, Zenith has consistently increased its share of the television market.

Zenith promotes hand-wiring aggressively in its advertising, and a good percentage of the service fraternity gives the brand its blessing. On the other hand, manufacturers like RCA, committed to printed circuitry, extol the benefits of "bonded space-age circuitry" and avoid using the term "printed circuit" in any connection at all. RCA points out that this is the same construction used in guided missiles, radar, and other supersophisticated electronics hardware. The premise is that if it is reliable enough for the space program and the military, it ought certainly to be reliable enough for consumer goods. While this is true and consumer equipment using printed circuits is, on the whole, dependable and efficient, the damage done by premature marketing of an unproven technology is still being felt in the market place.

With strides being made in the design, production, and reduced cost of solid-state devices such as transistors and diodes, the use of vacuum tubes in home electronics is diminishing. Magnavox has led the pack in this country in converting to all solid-state circuitry. Magnavox was the first to introduce a stereo-radio phonograph using no tubes at all, and was again the first in offering large-screen black-and-white television sets that were completely transistorized.

Here again, the manufacturer prematurely marketed an untried and unproven product. Early Magnavox solid-state television sets were so full of bugs that a service bulletin sent out to dealers listed nineteen major circuitry modifications needed to make the sets perform. These changes were costly and time-consuming and required above-average technical competence, since the repair of solid-state circuitry was strange to most servicemen. No compensation was ever offered by Magnavox to those who had to clean up the errors that should have been detected by the factory. The customers who bought these television sets had to endure the annoyance of putting up with substandard performance or being without them while they were sent back for modification.

Shortly after this fiasco, Magnavox instituted a program of setting up independent service agencies to handle the repair of solid-state television sets. This was the only way that Magnavox could restore the dealer's confidence in the product and relieve him of the burden of trying to service a new and very complicated type of circuitry.

Few manufacturers spend enough time testing new products at the plant before they are put into general distribution. Again and again defects show up after a product is delivered to the consumer that should have been caught before production was in full swing and the goods shipped out to dealers.

Most quality-control men at the factory level would welcome the opportunity for more thorough design studies, component checkout, and accelerated wear and aging test programs. However, the pressure to meet manufacturing deadlines prior to the annual or semiannual introduction of new models curtails testing and freezes designs before they are made as bugfree as possible.

Most manufacturers of home appliances, especially in the electronics field, depend upon the independent servicemen or factory-field service representatives to find the cures for inherent manufacturing defects. Malfunctions and breakdowns of specific components and circuits start cropping up all over the country. It is the lonely bench man, sweating over a customer's sick television set far into the night, who discovers the wrong-value resistor, the condenser wired to the wrong terminal, or a poorly soldered connection. Eventually some of this information filters to the factory, and that is how service bulletins are born. Sylvania, in its service bulletins, is generous enough to print the names of the servicemen who report the results of their trouble-shooting.

The failures due to poor design or faulty components are eventually diagnosed and the modifications made in a subsequent production. These changes or interim "fixes" are reflected in service bulletins that tell the service people what troubles to expect and how to fix a model bearing a serial number within a specified range. The bulletins go on to advise that in production subsequent to a certain serial the changes were incorporated in the product at the factory and those models will be all right.

The consumer who buys an appliance with a suspect serial number is never told about it. If the equipment fails, he is never advised that it was due to a manufacturing oversight. If the defect should show up after the warranty has expired, the customer will have to pay for the repairs even though the fault is one the manufacturer has acknowledged and since corrected on other models. What logic permits appliance and television manufacturers to shove their mistakes under the rug while the public interest has brought about the disclosure of similar errors in the automobile industry?

3

Nobody Else Is
Complaining

THE COMPANIES that produce major appliances and home electronics seem to have the production problem licked. Their factories can pour out a flood of goods ranging from heavy, bulky appliances to ultra-sophisticated small-screen color television sets. Although all of this equipment is highly complicated and requires a great amount of specialized design, tooling, and machinery, shortages never seem to last very long. Miracles are achieved in bringing to market, in the shortest possible time, huge quantities of these varied and complex products.

Distribution methods have been streamlined for maximum efficiency. Computers make it possible to locate models, check availability, and place orders in seconds. The computer will subtract orders from inventory, direct shipments, and send bills, keeping track of every piece by model and serial number.

It is only when the equipment needs service that the industry cannot claim the same efficiency and performance that it has achieved in production and distribution.

Major appliance service is handled by the manufacturer in one of two ways. In the first, he sells his product to a dealer with the cost of service during the warranty period "outboarded" in the price of the item. This means that on top of the wholesale cost of a refrigerator or other appliance a store is charged an added fee for service, which will be from five to fifteen dollars depending upon the complexity of the unit. This is service the dealer expects the manufacturer to perform with his own factory-operated service department or by an independent service agency selected and approved by the factory. Many factories, such as Westinghouse and Whirlpool, "inboard" the service fee and a dealer does not know how much the warranty charge has added to the cost of the goods. Where the service is prebilled and there is no factory or authorized service agency available, the dealer who operates his own service department is permitted to charge the manufacturer for labor performed during the warranty period by the dealer's own personnel.

Factory-owned service departments came into being for several logical and urgent reasons. In the early 1950's it became apparent that the dealer-service structure could not, by itself, handle the rising service load brought about by the expansion of the industry. Population growth and the formation of new households foreshadowed a burgeoning market.

This period also saw the development of the mass-merchandisers and discount department stores. Chains such as E. J. Korvette, Two Guys, Grand-Way, K-Mart, Woolco, J. M. Fields, White Front Stores, and Zayre's were opening new stores from coast to coast. While manufacturers publicly decried the price-cutting tactics of the discounters to their regular dealers, privately they saw the discounter as a source of huge volume. Whatever a factory may say about protecting the position of the independent dealer in his market, the name of the game is still Volume. Factories fight one another fiercely for "market penetration" and sales managers arrive and depart upon "percentage of industry" figures.

Discounting seemed to be an ideal means of moving large quantities of goods through fewer outlets and thus reducing distribution costs. These huge chains brought carloads of merchandise directly into their own warehouses and eliminated for the manufacturer the costs of warehousing, shipment of single pieces, and the commissions paid to salesmen calling on individual stores to pick up piecemeal orders.

Since these mass merchandisers were promotion-oriented and were primarily concerned with selling in big quantities, their concept of low-overhead operation did not permit them the luxury of operating their own service departments. (In fact, Grand-Way does not even have a listed telephone number, so service calls cannot be phoned to the stores.) The factories then stepped in and developed their own service operations to relieve the discount chains of service responsibility and permit the chains to concentrate their efforts on sales.

Most factories are now trying to market their major appliances using the prebilled-service method. From their standpoint, charging extra for an intangible like service immediately gives them substantial added revenue. They know that an occasional appliance will need an inordinate amount of service, but by spreading the risk over a great number of units they will average out at a profit. No manufacturer has claimed that he is losing money by charging for service and operating his own service company.

In markets of high population density the major manufacturers maintain their own service shops and repair men to handle both in-warranty and out-of-warranty service on their products. In theory, this is a good system. Dealers are relieved of the expense of maintaining parts inventories, hiring service people, operating service vehicles, and routing calls. The customer is also supposed to benefit because the factory service people have to be familiar with the foibles of only one make and are expected to stock the parts that have been found to be susceptible to frequent breakdown.

When this setup is working smoothly, everybody is happy. The dealer delivers the appliance and divorces himself from the customer by telling him to call the service company if the item breaks down. The customer places the service call, it is handled promptly by a courteous technician who gets right to the trouble, fixes it, says, "It was only this little widget!" and cleans up after himself and leaves.

This would be an ideal situation and would, if it prevailed nationally, give no justification for the bad image the industry has acquired. Unfortunately, factory service has its drawbacks. The factories have as much difficulty recruiting and training competent service people as any other industry. The shortage of service personnel was so acute that recently the Hartford, Connecticut, branch of the General Electric Service Division was trying to catch up with a backlog of twelve hundred service calls.

In New York City and other major markets covered by factory-owned service companies, it is practically impossible to register a service complaint on an air conditioner on a hot summer day. Consumers dialing service companies have gotten nothing but busy signals or no answer for periods of up to two weeks.

These large service organizations are also vulnerable

34

to labor disputes. A strike of five hundred greater New York and Connecticut servicemen against General Electric and Hotpoint in May 1969 lasted eighteen days. In Philadelphia four hundred Sears television and appliance servicemen struck for almost two weeks in April 1969, and tied up deliveries and service as the truckers refused to cross the servicemen's picket lines.

An appliance owner waiting for service from a factory-owned service company has no one but an answering service to tell his troubles to. If he goes back to the store where he bought he may get sympathy, but very little actual help. The dealer has abdicated his responsibility in favor of the factory and has no facilities of his own to see the problem through.

When the manufacturer has no service facilities of his own but has contracted with the dealer to see that service is taken care of for the prebilled fee, this function is farmed out by the manufacturer to an independent service agency. The independent service agency may comprise anything from a single individual working part time out of his garage to a large well-staffed service specialist. These service companies usually contract with several makers to handle in-warranty service on their products. Service calls are routed to them by the dealer or, in some cases, the customer is instructed to call them directly. They are reimbursed by the factory, either by a flat contract fee covering the warranty period or by billing the factory on a per-call basis. Few service companies are large enough to handle a volume of contract work that would permit them to spread the risk as widely as the factory can. They are reluctant to do contract service and try to expend the minimum effort on it. Usually, if they have to make more than one service call on an appliance covered by contract, they have lost money on that contract.

On a per-call basis, they make out slightly better except that the factories have set up maximum charges for different kinds of repair operations. In most cases these payments have become unrealistic in today's labor market. The usual factory labor allowance for changing a refrigerator compressor will range from $12.50 to $25. Most good refrigeration men feel that $35 is the least that such a job should be worth. Appliance owners have waited days during the peak summer season with a non-functioning refrigerator or air conditioner while the independent refrigeration men were taking care of the more lucrative commercial and nonwarranty jobs.

The second method of handling appliance service is for the factory to sell the merchandise to a so-called servicing dealer without a prebilled charge for service. Under this arrangement the dealer absorbs all labor costs during the warranty period. The quality of dealer-owned service departments can range from very good to very bad. Where an independent appliance dealer does a substantial volume of business in his market, receives a fair price for his goods, and is a well-established member of the community in which he trades, he is more likely to take his service responsibility seriously. These stores struggle to maintain a good service image as their only weapon against the discount stores.

They cannot always offer the lowest prices, the widest selections, or the most convenient locations. What they try to do is give their customer a feeling of genuine interest in his purchase and follow up the sale with prompt attention to his problems. This type of retailer is becoming a rare bird as good service people are not being developed fast enough and the cost of correcting factory "boo-boos" becomes intolerable.

This problem was discussed by Jack Boring, a dealer in Kansas City, Missouri, whose $6-million-a-year appliance business was built on personalized service. Mr. Boring was quoted in the April 16, 1969, issue of *Home Furnishings Daily*:

"Too many manufacturers regard the dealer as an extension of their own assembly lines.

"They expect the dealer to make repairs and adjustments on products that should have been shipped from the plant perfect in the first place."

Boring declared that producers shouldn't expect this any longer because the retailer has all he can do to take care of his own service operations.

"The high price tag on labor has driven our service costs sky high," he said. "What's needed in this industry right now are controls over what the manufacturers can expect from the servicing retailer. It's unrealistic to expect that merchants can provide the type of services with today's margins that they did on the fat profits of yesterday."

The reliance upon a dealer's own service efforts as a means of survival was expressed by Carroll McMullen, a Toledo appliance dealer and past president of the National Appliance and Radio/Television Dealers' Association (NARDA). McMullen's address to the NARDA School of Service Management was reported by *Home Furnishings Daily* on May 7, 1969:

"Good, fast personalized service is now replacing the lowest price in town as the motivating factor for consumers to buy at a particular store.

37

"Personalized service, good fast service, is truly the only weapon available for independent appliance-TV dealers with a volume of under $500,000 to compete with the discount giants and with the great Sears, Roebuck as well as high-volume, low margin discounters.

"These giants," he said, "generally hold all the high cards, like plenty of capital, managerial talent in depth, electronic data accounting for controls that the small dealer many times doesn't even consider, and the beautiful ace of hearts represented by purchasing power with all the side benefits, despite the Federal Trade Commission saying that everyone must be treated equally."

When an independent appliance dealer cannot afford good repair men on his payroll or does not have access to competent and reliable outside agencies, things can get very bad for the customer. Service complaints get stalled, handled incompetently, or just ignored. It is the responsibility of the factory, when it starts to get a playback of factory-addressed complaints from such a dealer's customers, to either upgrade his service or drop him as an outlet.

This rarely happens. Regardless of how small his sales may be, he is still some salesman's customer and is adding units to the district's sales figures. Only when a dealer is unable to pay for his goods and is no sales factor is the franchise revoked.

What happens when a consumer is frustrated in his efforts to receive service from the factory branch, service agency, or dealer? The only recourse most appliance owners have is a letter to the factory. These letters pour in to the manufacturers every day. They unfold tales of constant breakdown and repair of the same appliance, weeks waiting for parts while washing piles up, food spoils, and television screens stare back blankly.

The manufacturers have a staff of people in their customer-relations departments to reply to this torrent of grief. Replies are sent to the complaining customer sympathizing with his problem, assuring him of the basic soundness of the product and promising that the complaint will be followed up. Carbon copies of this letter plus photostats of the customer's letter to the factory are then sent to the dealer who sold the product or the service agency responsible. These banal "Who, me?" letters from the manufacturers to the unhappy consumers came in for criticism by Ezra Kuhn, senior projects analyst for the President's Committee on Consumer Interests. Speaking in Philadelphia to a group of service representatives in May 1969, he gave the following as a typical reply to a consumer complaint to the factory:

"We sell to independent wholesale dealers who sell to thousands of independent retailers of their choice. Under this system of distribution, the problems you describe are handled locally by dealers or the nearest distributor. We certainly appreciate your bringing this to our attention, and you will very shortly be contacted by the distributor or his representative."

This hand-washing technique just throws the ball back to the same people who were unable to take care of the problem initially. If they had been able to, the customer would not have been driven to seek relief from the factory.

Factory follow-up to these letters is generally haphazard or lacking entirely unless further correspondence is received from the customer. All factories have district service managers whose duties include training servicemen in their particular products and trouble-shooting complaints of a nonroutine nature. Eventually, a long-standing gripe may be referred to a district service manager. Like a consulting neurosurgeon he will make an appointment to examine an ailing appliance either in a customer's home or at the dealer's shop. Hopefully, if a complaint has progressed that far, something gets done.

In the case of a complaint directed solely against the performance of a particular dealer, the customer's letter is usually referred to the wholesale representative who calls on the dealer. Since the dealer is the salesman's customer, the salesman's follow-up usually takes the form of, "Say, Bob, what are you doing about Mrs. What's-Her-Name's reefer?" The salesman isn't about to alienate his account by taking a hard line with the man who helps pay for his kid's orthodontia. The dealer just has to say that he is doing all he can, and the subject changes.

It is due more, perhaps, to the huge volume of factory-directed complaints than to a real lack of concern on the part of the manufacturers that these letters do not bring about any direct or dramatic cures. All appliance manufacturers worry about the monster that product service represents. All of them conduct periodic training sessions for service technicians all over the country. They publish product-information manuals and bulletins to which their servicing dealers are obliged to subscribe and for which the factories charge a fee.

It is only since the service scandal has attracted attention in Washington and is being discussed more openly in trade journals such as *Home Furnishings Daily* and the public press that the manufacturers are devoting more intensive efforts to the issue. Companies like Westinghouse and Philco-Ford have transferred top executive talent from sales to service responsibility, hoping to upgrade the segment of their operation that had previously been an orphan. Yet the top salaries still go to sales managers, the men who move the merchandise from the factory to the retail floors—not to the engineers or service managers, who have to make it work.

Sears, Roebuck & Co. is the largest single retailer of appliances in this country. In market after market, Sears claims from 20 to 40 percent of industry volume. Its impact on the appliance business is so great that giants like General Electric, Frigidaire, and Westinghouse develop special models of washing machines, dryers, refrigerators, freezers, and other appliances, with which their dealers are supposed to "fight Sears."

Discussion here will deal only with Sears' service. The merchandising techniques that have made them dominant will be taken up later.

Sears' service setup is very similar to a factory-owned service operation. Sears is concerned only with its own Coldspot, Kenmore, and Silvertone brands. Most of these products are made by factories in which Sears has a substantial or controlling interest. This permits Sears to have a great deal to say about how an appliance is styled and constructed and how much it should cost.

Since Sears is paying for its own service it would behoove it to try to make its appliances as foolproof as possible. However, Sears is governed by the same limitations of production expediency and cost reduction as anyone else. Its products do "conk out" and require service in the customer's home as frequently as most other companies' do.

Sears' record for fast, efficient service up to this point has been excellent in some markets and very poor in others. In spite of apparent efforts to upgrade and improve its service image, hundreds of independent appliance dealers all over the country stay in business and make a living selling to unhappy Sears customers. This is not to say that all Sears service is bad, but in an operation so vast it would be miraculous to keep everyone satisfied.

It would be prudent for a consumer contemplating the purchase of a major appliance from Sears to make some inquiries first. Neighbors, fellow workers, and friends should be queried as to their experience with the quality of the service the local Sears store has given them. It should not be taken for granted that because Sears is so huge their service is always first rate. The same inquiries should be made wherever possible about any appliance dealer with whom the buyer has not had previous experience.

If, as Newton Minow, former chairman of the Federal Communications Commission, has claimed, television programing is a vast wasteland, the repair of television sets in this country must be an enormous quicksand. The Better Business Bureaus probably receive more complaints about inept, dishonest, or overpriced television service than for any other reason. The shady tactics or incompetent work performed by some TV repairmen have made all television service suspect. The honest, technically informed television serviceman is tarred with the same brush as the ignorant or dishonest "shoe clerk."

The concern here is how television service is managed by the factories, distributors, and dealers. For purposes of concision, my discussion of television service will encompass the service of all home electronic equipment such as radios, phonographs, and tape recorders, as well as black-and-white and color television.

Of all the television manufacturers, only RCA has

established a network of nationwide factory-owned service depots. RCA has operated its service company for over twenty years, and it covers most of the important marketing and high-density-population areas in the United States. Where this service is available to RCA set owners it is generally advisable to use it. The only reason not to would be if a set owner had sufficient confidence that his local repairman would be cheaper, faster, and more competent than RCA. All of these criteria are perfectly possible to meet, because RCA service throughout the country is not always prompt and never cheap, and as RCA's turnover of personnel is substantial, it is sometimes not as proficient as would be desirable. But unless the RCA set owner has a blood relative or lodge brother for a serviceman, RCA service should be considered his best bet.

Except in the largest markets like New York, Los Angeles, Chicago, and Philadelphia, the other television manufacturers have not made any appreciable penetration into the service end of the business. Unless a television-set buyer lives where central factory service is available for a certain make, he will have to get along with the service furnished by the store from which he purchased his equipment.

This presents the buyer with service of a very variable quality. A large television and appliance specialty store that is franchised for nationally recognized brands is apt to have as well-staffed and efficient a service department as can be found anywhere. The big discount department stores will use central factory service where available or turn the service of their sets over to independent service companies.

Manufacturers will pay independent service shops to furnish in-warranty service, usually for a period of ninety days from purchase, on all home electronic products except color television. If a radio or phonograph is brought into their shop, they will repair it and charge the manufacturer for the service.

On television sets, the manufacturer does not underwrite the cost of service during the 90-day warranty period except when this service is prebilled to the dealer in a manner similar to major appliance repairs.

In the case of color television, which is the biggest service problem in the electronics field, service agencies will charge the dealer for the initial setup and subsequent service calls on a flat-rate-per-call basis. An alternative arrangement is that a service company will insist on a flat contract fee of twenty to thirty dollars for the setup and maintenance of a color television set for a dealer for the first ninety days of operation.

Some television manufacturers have taken steps to provide some degree of uniformity and control over color television servicing at least during the first ninety days of ownership. Philco and Admiral have initiated a program of prebilling or in-boarding the cost of ninety-day service to dealers on each television set that they buy. This increased cost is intended to be passed on to the customer with the usual markup. For this added cost the manufacturer obliges himself to provide either in-home service on consoles or carry-in service on portables. This is accomplished by the setting up of independent television servicemen as factory-authorized service stations.

The arrangement is supposed to give the customer an iron-clad assurance of service availability at least for the initial ninety-day period. It would presumably protect a buyer whether he bought his set from a television specialist or a department or discount store, or even mail order. A service agency performing repairs on a new TV set will bill the factory for its labor according to rate schedules established by the manufacturer. Since the factory has already collected for contingent service on every set it produces, it makes no difference which service station sends in a bill on any particular set. They will honor claims only for the first ninety days and will use the customer's warranty card to verify the purchase date. These warranty cards are attached to a new product and are supposed to be filled out and mailed back to the factory within ten days after the set is delivered.

All this presupposes that competent, trained people are readily available to service the product in whatever part of the country it is sold. This is very difficult to achieve. In many rural markets there are very few technicians, and most of them are dealers in a small way for at least one brand of television. They are not going to put themselves out to service a set that some wiseguy in their market bought at a discount store in a city a few miles away.

Metropolitan specialists who do nothing but service work are in demand by practically every maker of home electronic gear. They are generally so overloaded with work that repairs cannot be handled as promptly as everyone would wish.

Many color television set buyers who are worried about getting proper service have purchased their color sets from service-dealers. These outlets are primarily a one- or two-man service operation which handles a minimum of brands. They cater to their regular service customers or make a sale when they have an old television chassis apart on the bench and tell the customer that it is not worth fixing. Some of these outlets do a very respectable color television business and such a business, properly run, can be extremely profitable. They are usually in small, low-rent locations with some men operating out of their homes, basements, or garages. Service-dealers do not do much advertising, and they are equipped to make a profit on the sets they take as trade-ins. Unless they are foolish enough to try to compete with the giants on prices, they can make a very comfortable living.

From the consumer's standpoint, there are several disadvantages in buying a set from the small service-dealer. First, his selection is usually limited in terms of brands offered and models shown. Sets are frequently ordered from catalogues since the dealer is not financed well enough to stock many expensive color television sets. Secondly, if they begin to sell in any quantity at all, the one- or two-man shop quickly becomes bogged down with service. It does not have the manpower to cope with both regular service work and the upkeep on the sets it has sold. Sets begin to pile up on the workshop floor and customers begin waiting days and weeks for their television sets to be repaired and returned.

Promises of instant service are always suspect. Here, if one is willing to take the trouble, inquiries can be made of the local Better Business Bureau or Chamber of Commerce. These agencies keep files on the consumer complaints they have received in their area. Reference to these files should pinpoint the outlets that seem to give more grief than others.

Just as important in home-appliance repair as the supply of proficient service personnel is the availability of replacement parts. Nothing frustrates a serviceman trying to complete a job more than having to tell a customer over and over, "Your parts are on order." A customer staring at a blank television screen, taking her dirty laundry out to the laundromat, or keeping her milk in the neighbor's refrigerator shrieks, "Where does it have to come from? I've been waiting four weeks!"

If a part involved in the primary function of an appliance or television set does not arrive from a parts depot in a week or less, a customer is advised that the order must have been forwarded to the "factory." This involves further delay and raises temperatures all around.

A dealer or serviceman must order parts for in-warranty repairs from an authorized factory parts depot, distributor, or, in a very few cases, the factory itself. The servicing agency is billed for the parts ordered plus shipping charges. In order to receive credit for parts that are still in guarantee, the defective parts must be returned to the depot tagged with a form that requires almost as much information as a title search. The serviceman must give make, model, serial number, customer's name and address, date of installation, date of replacement, and the nature of the part failure. Sometimes, in order to receive credit, he must also list the date and invoice number on which he was charged for the replacement parts. This is a tedious, time-consuming, and expensive chore, but unless it is done promptly and according to each manufacturer's distinct and different method, credits may be held up or forfeited entirely.

Some manufacturers have made enlightened progress toward reducing the snarl of red tape surrounding the ordering and returning of parts. The Magic Chef Company, which makes gas and electric ranges, requires only that parts be returned with a copy of the shipping ticket in the box in which they were received. They will ship free of charge almost any part of their own manufacture. Parts such as porcelain door and side panels, burner grates, glass backguards, panels, and control knobs are supplied free without too much regard to the age of the appliance.

The stocking of an ample supply of quickly available replacement parts is a function over which the factory has a great deal of control, and one for which it can be charged with direct responsibility. For this reason, access to replacement parts has improved significantly in the past few years. Most factories have set up fewer but more complete parts depots across the country. In a well-run parts depot the orders should be shipped no later than the day after they are received, and if United Parcel Service is used, can be delivered the next day.

Area parts depots cannot be expected to stock every trim part, escutcheon, or chrome strip for every model made in the past ten years or more. They should be expected to supply promptly the structural and functional parts without which an appliance cannot operate. A presidential task force on consumer protection has recommended that manufacturers have in the hands of parts depots and service agencies parts, parts lists, and repair manuals for all new models before they are in distribution. In addition, the government has asked the industry to determine how many years parts for a particular model should be available for the repair of consumer appliances. Planning to shut off the supply of replacement parts five or ten years after original manufacture helps build accelerated obsolescence into the product at the time it is produced.

If a housewife has to tie a rope around her refrigerator because of a broken door latch or if she has to bail out her automatic washer with a coffee can because the pump is gone, she does not want to be told after two or three weeks, "Your parts are on order," or, "Sorry, they don't make them any more."

4

My Old One Lasted
Twenty Years

UNLIKE THE persistent and inexorable rise of the prices of just about every commodity and service purchased today, the prices of major appliances have actually declined in the past twenty years. In this period we have experienced the reduced buying power of the dollar, a much higher cost of living, and appreciably higher labor and raw-material costs. In spite of this, appliance prices are lower today than twenty years ago. This is especially true if we take into account the additional features and the added capacities and conveniences now offered.

Twenty years ago three-hundred dollars was the going price for an automatic washer, a twelve-cubic-foot non-frostless refrigerator or a ten-inch black and white television set. Dryers were substantially over two-hundred dollars, as was any decent gas or electric range or single-speed, monaural console phonograph.

Today, three-hundred dollars buys a sixteen- or seventeen-cubic-foot, two-door, frost-free refrigerator, a portable eighteen-inch color television set, or three twelve-inch black-and-white portable television sets. It is unnecessary to spend more than two-hundred dollars for a two-speed automatic washer; a good dryer should cost no more than $150, and for two-hundred dollars electric ranges are now offered with self-cleaning ovens.

The reason the consumer is getting more for his money is not simply the use of cheaper materials, engineering and production shortcuts, automation, or improved overall efficiency on the part of the manufacturers. Appliance manufacturers would dearly love to get higher prices for their products. The industry, with the exception of some specialized manufacturers like Maytag, has not been able either to operate its consumer-products divisions in the black or to make the kind of profits that are made with similar investments elsewhere.

A breakdown of the profit or loss of the home-appliance divisions of such diversified companies as General Electric, Westinghouse, American Motors, General Motors, or Philco-Ford is not available outside the offices of these companies. Nevertheless, from time to time, statements are made in trade journals or the financial pages that indicate that these divisions have lost money. We do not know the accounting methods used to arrive at these figures or the amounts of corporate overhead with which the appliance operation is burdened.

Nevertheless, it is a matter of record that after a period of losses, Philco sold out to Ford, the Kelvinator Division of American Motors was bought by White Consolidated Industries, and the Norge Division of Borg-Warner was sold to Fedders Corporation.

Competition is the major factor keeping the prices of appliances lower than the corporate directors and stockholders would like to see them. The price structure of the industry is established by the leaders. These major producers control so large a portion of the market that their mass-production economies can make possible lower unit costs; price reductions or lower margins can be absorbed within the corporate entity. This puts a continuous squeeze on the smaller companies. They either become more efficient in order to exist, or become unprofitable to the point where they either sell out or close up.

Every time Frigidaire, General Electric, or RCA reduces a price by five dollars, sales managers and production engineers of competing factories stay up all night sharpening pencils so that their price can be shaved by ten dollars. Even in the case of price hikes, the factories play follow the leader. The July 22, 1968, issue of *Home Furnishings Daily* announced a 5 percent increase in the wholesale price of General Electric's appliances, and the paragraph below advised that Philco-Ford's prices were being raised by 4 percent.

The need to stay competitive or to absorb rises in the cost of labor and material spurs the design and engineering staffs to search out less costly components or more economical manufacturing methods. The increased use of plastics as a cost saver is obvious to anyone who has recently examined almost any appliance, television set, or console stereo. Customers shopping for a refrigerator are sometimes shocked when they realize that all refrigerator inner door liners are now made of one large molded plastic sheet. This has been true for quite a while, and regardless of how much the customer is willing to spend, no other material is presently being used for this function.

Plastic door shelves, egg containers, and vegetable-crisper drawer covers are endemic. Occasionally, even the complete vegetable and meat bins themselves are plastic. All of Admiral's refrigerator and freezer food-compartment liners, with the exception of the Duplex line, are plastic, as are the liners of Kelvinator's Trimwall series of refrigerators. A vigorous research program was recently undertaken by the Norge Division of Borg-Warner to develop an all-plastic refrigerator cabinet made of Marbon, a plastic manufactured by yet another division of Borg-Warner.

Significant savings have been realized in the production of cabinets housing home electronic equipment. In every manufacturer's line of big-screen color television sets, the lowest-priced models are housed in metal cabinets. A plastic cabinet would cost less, and the only reason steel is still used for this purpose is that a plastic has not been found that is strong enough to handle the weight and withstand the heat generated by a large screen color television set. Now that plastics are found housing small-screen (ten- to fifteen-inch diagonal measurement) color television, it remains to be proven how well they will resist warpage from heat.

It is becoming increasingly rare to find a portable black-and-white television set in anything but a plastic cabinet. A domestically made AM-FM table radio in a wood cabinet is almost impossible to find at a reasonable price.

The award for ingenuity and courage for cabinet design should go to the people who conceived of using plastic instead of wood in large television and stereo furniture. The entire fronts of expensive Magnavox television sets, stereo phonographs, and TV-stereo combinations are made completely of plastic. Intricate carvings and subtle woodlike finishes are applied so artfully that few are aware of the true nature of the material used unless attention is called to it. While opinions may vary as to the durability of these plastic parts, there is no question but that they are there to save the manufacturer money.

Magnavox owns several furniture factories and continues to acquire more. These include one devoted exclusively to the production of large plastic cabinets and components, while Philco-Ford is operating a plant for the electronics and furniture industry, producing cabinets that are quite massive and are made almost entirely of plastic.

This is not meant as a wholesale condemnation of the use of plastics in home appliances. But there is ample reason for the consumer to be wary of their excessive use as they supersede metals and woods in more and more applications. Many buyers complained of cracked door liners in their refrigerators shortly after they were delivered; this was caused by either imperfectly molded liners or the inability of the large panels to resist slight stress or warpage over a large surface. Freezer owners in particular have had to replace many cracked bottom breaker strips (the plastic pieces that join the inner and outer shell on a refrigerator or freezer). The strip breaks when a frozen package is accidentally dropped on it, because, being very cold, it is extremely brittle and cracks easily.

The use of plastic in place of porcelain on steel for lining the interior of refrigerators does not make much difference in the operation of the box. In fact, it could be argued that the plastic has better insulating characteristics. However, repairs to tubing leaks are vastly more difficult, and some manufacturers even offer to replace the refrigerator if the liner cracks or if it becomes necessary to get to the insulation for service. Whether the plastic inner surfaces will maintain their color, resist absorbing odors, or remain as perfectly smooth and nonporous as porcelain is still a question that will take a few more years to answer.

The use of plastics in console television and stereo cabinets does not detract from the performance of these products. It has made possible the mass production of highly styled units in an endless variety of designs and simulated finishes. Not having to rely on hand craftsmanship in the finish of these cabinets has brought substantial benefits to manufacturers. However, the savings have not been passed on to the consumer by any substantial reduction in the selling price. The fronts of current television and stereo models selling for upwards of five hundred dollars in many popular makes are plastic, whereas previously all-wood cabinets were available for the same money. Manufacturers and retailers are still defensive about the use of plastics. This can be seen from the fact that nowhere in the advertising or retail sales pitch is the use of plastics touted as an advantage to the consumer. Few retail salesmen will volunteer the information that the refrigerator you are thinking about buying is lined with plastic or that the front of the gorgeous Spanish-style stereo is not really hand-carved wood.

Another example of using less expensive materials is the substitution of aluminum for copper in the refrigerator and condenser coils of some refrigerators. A sprayed-on vinyl coating instead of porcelain on the inside of dishwashers is used by General Electric and others. The side panels of some ranges are painted with enamel rather than finished with the same baked-on porcelain as the rest of the stove. The same is true of the interior surface of the clothes drum of Norge, Whirlpool and Kenmore dryers.

There are basic disadvantages to the consumer in these production money savers. Aluminum is not as efficient a cold conductor as copper and is more difficult to work with if a refrigerator needs repair. Vinyl dishwasher liners are subject to discoloration from excessive heat and from the chemicals that may be in the water supply. Enamel stove panels will discolor and become scratched, while porcelain parts will not. The constant tumbling of clothes in an enamel dryer drum causes abrasion of the finish, and eventually rust spots can appear.

Another means of controlling appliance production costs is the freezing of basic cabinet and design features. Manufacturers use the same dies to stamp outer steel cabinet shells year in and year out. The last time there was a significant change in the cabinet design of refrigerators was the switch from rounded tops and bulging fronts to the flat-top, squared-off look seen today.

When model-year changes must be made, it is the stylist, not the engineer, who has the most to do. Chrome strips are run horizontally rather than vertically, pasted-on vinyl panels are reduced in size or made larger or their colors varied. Interior colors of refrigerators change each year from yellow to various shades of blue and green. Backsplash panels on washers, dryers, and ranges are altered enough to make their appearance distinct from the previous year's models.

The cost of television sets and other home electronic equipment has been most reduced by improved technology and materials. Radical changes in the state of the art came about quickly due to the more sophisticated components and techniques developed for military hardware being rapidly applied to consumer products. The spur to improve reliability, increase performance, save weight, and miniaturize components is provided by huge research projects financed in large measure by the armed forces and the space program.

The incorporation of printed circuitry, transistorization of circuits, solid-state power supplies, and integrated circuits into home electronics products is a by-product of this research. These changes are revolutionary and should benefit the consumer in terms of fewer product failures, better performance, more compact cabinetry, and lower costs.

The substantial economies achieved by electronics manufacturers in production are not reflected by a discernible downward price tendency. This is because the savings made in the cost of components and more efficient manufacturing techniques are offset by increased labor and marketing costs.

The factor of greatest concern to both the manufacturer and the purchaser of a home appliance is how the product will stand up under use. The manufacturer is not anxious to have his product fall apart or become so troublesome in the field as to create an odor from which the company's reputation will permanently suffer. This happened to the people who made Jacob's Launderall, an automatic washing machine that appeared immediately after World War II.

Appliance dealers after the war, hungry for something to sell and with customers anxious to spend money on durable goods after a five-year famine, snapped up these washers as fast as they could be made.

Their failure is history and due, perhaps, as much to inherent faulty design as to component malfunction. In the Launderall the clothes were loaded from the top into a perforated basket. This basket rested in an outer watertight tub. The washing action was accomplished by the inner tub rocking back and forth inside the outer tub and providing the needed agitation. These machines broke down all over the country and the inability of service people to make them run caused dealers to stop buying them and the company to go out of business.

The Bendix Appliance Company made a costly marketing blunder in 1948, when it unveiled a "revolutionary" new type of automatic washer, the Bendix Economat. This machine washed the clothes using a conventional back-and-forth agitator. Its departure from all other automatic washers was the manner in which the water was extracted. The universal method is to spin the wash basket inside an outer tub at high speed. Centrifugal force drives the water out of the clothes, with the degree of dryness dependent upon the rpm of the spin.

In the Economat only one tub was used, and this was made of a flexible synthetic-rubber material. In order to extract the water, a pump evacuated the air inside the tub. This caused the walls of the tub to collapse against the agitator column and the clothes, thus squeezing the water out.

The advantages were freedom from the vibration ordinarily caused by the spinning; the fact that no special plumbing was required as the machine could be hooked up to a kitchen faucet or filled with a hose or bucket; and cheapness. Two models were available for $149.95 and $189.95, depending upon whether they filled and regulated their own water temperature automatically or not.

This machine was made by a pioneer in automatic home laundry equipment, and at that time, perhaps the largest manufacturer of it. Besides, the Economat filled a need. More people could afford to own an automatic washer, and machines could be sold without expensive plumbing work and used above the basement since they did not have to be bolted to the floor.

Unfortunately, the Economat did not work out. Articles left in clothes, like a screwdriver or a nail in a workman's pocket, would puncture the tub. Pumps and seals failed to maintain the needed vacuum and were constantly being replaced. So many of the machines were sold and were the source of so much grief that the repercussions damaged Bendix's position in the entire market. Soon after this episode Bendix sold out to Philco, and the new Philco-Bendix Division wisely discontinued production of the Economat.

Even present-day giants come out with badly conceived or inadequately engineered products. Several years ago Frigidaire marketed a Cold-Wall refrigerator. In this model the refrigerator coils were concealed behind the food-compartment liner and embedded next to the insulation. This was supposed to do away with unsightly evaporator coils and plates inside the box and provide more storage space. But under high humidity conditions, moisture would condense on the refrigerator liner surfaces and the walls would sweat. In addition, after a period of time, the insulation would absorb moisture from the coils and become soaked, water would seep from the space between the inner and outer walls, and the insulation would be rendered useless.

A few years ago, Magnavox started shipping a new color-television chassis on which Channel 8 could not be properly received. At the point where the best sound and picture could be tuned, a herringbone pattern appeared on the screen. When Magnavox was made aware of the problem, the solution it devised involved the replacement of a complete I.F. (Interharmonic Frequency) printed circuit board with associated tubes and components.

Early Sylvania eighteen-inch portable color television sets experienced a similar herringbone pattern on Channel 3. Sylvania never came up with a practical correction and just hoped the problem would disappear.

Even RCA Victor, the color-television pioneer and leading producer, is not immune. The most expensive models in the 1967 line used the so-called Mark III chassis. It featured a tuner with automatic fine tuning for color and rapid tuning of UHF channels. This system failed to perform as expected, and later production the same year substituted the less expensive Mark II chassis in the same-model cabinets at no reduction in the wholesale or retail price.

The lesson for the consumer from this recital of manufacturing fluffs is to avoid buying either completely new products or distinct departures from previously proven models the first year they are offered. The customer who asks a salesman for a particular make of refrigerator because "My old one lasted twenty years!" is generally due for a disappointment.

Modern appliances are so much more complex that it would be economically impossible for a manufacturer to construct them to outlast the relatively simple and unsophisticated models they are replacing, without pricing the product out of the market. The industry has access to statistics on the average life span of an appliance. Because these figures show the life of an automatic washer to be 7.3 years does not mean that an owner who finds that she has to replace one after five and a half years got stuck. Life expectancy of appliances, like any other mechanical equipment, depends to a large degree upon reasonable maintenance and the type of usage to which it is subjected. An automatic washing machine will not last as long with a large family that requires the washing of several loads of laundry a day as it will where there are no small children and it is used perhaps once or twice a week. Placing a washer or dryer in a damp basement also tends to shorten its life.

A modern two-door refrigerator carries a much bigger load and performs many more functions than the old single-door models. The old boxes were cooled by a small across-the-top freezer section or a U-shaped evaporator that was used only for keeping trays of ice cubes and had to be defrosted when frost built up to the point where the inside looked like a miniature igloo. A new family-sized refrigerator should provide a freezing compartment with a separate door capable of maintaining a temperature of zero degrees to 10 degrees Fahrenheit, with a capacity of three to nine cubic feet. The fresh-food storage area will have a capacity of from ten to thirteen cubic feet and hold temperatures between 36 and 42 degrees. Some refrigerators also have a third zone for keeping meat fresh up to a week at a temperature just above freezing. Automatic ice makers are becoming more evident as manufacturers have been successful in promoting this extra-cost gadget. All these features involve vastly more complicated systems requiring additional fans, timers, heaters, and sensors.

It will take several more years for the reports on the

longevity of the big, multifunction refrigeration units to be significant. But it would be extremely optimistic to believe that the majority could remain trouble-free for any extended period of time.

A good gas range should outlive its buyer, and will if it is given reasonable care and kept decently clean. An electric range can now be expected to last longer than formerly. The primary cause for scrapping an electric range has been burnout of oven, broiler, or burner heating coils. The life expectancy of electric ranges has been greatly increased by the use of improved coils and heating elements.

Almost 100 percent of all portable or table radios, portable or console phonographs, tape recorders, and walkie-talkies made today are solid-state or tubeless. Black-and-white portable television and some console models use few or no tubes. A color television set is the most complicated and technically sophisticated piece of equipment ever mass-produced for the American consumer. Its service requirements have become greater, more technically demanding, and certainly more expensive as six or seven million sets are added to the burden every year. The only hope of avoiding complete chaos in this industry is to develop and employ more and more solid-state circuitry. The color-television manufacturers are now using solid-state devices to take over the function of tubes in various circuits. Motorola was the first to market a big-screen color television set that employs only one tube, the rest of the circuits being all solid state.

The wave of the future in the color-television industry is the exclusive use of easily removable and replaceable plug-in modules or prewired circuit boards controlling the separate operations of the set. This means that if a serviceman finds that a color television set has no sound or color, he has merely to remove the circuit module causing that symptom and plug in a new one. All this can be done without removing a chassis to the service shop, testing tubes, trouble-shooting for specific component failure, or even using service instruments or a soldering iron. The result is that less highly trained people will be able to cope with color-television service, and sets will rarely have to take a ride to the television-repair shop. The all-solid-state, or tubeless, color TV is the consumer's best hope that this expensive home-entertainment equipment will perform reliably for the number of years the large investment warrants.

In the home-electronics field the hopes for longer life and trouble-free operation become brighter and brighter. The use of transistors and other solid-state devices instead of vacuum tubes has dramatically improved reliability and longevity; circuits require lower operating voltages and run much cooler. The heat generated by vacuum tubes caused neighboring components such as resistors and condensers to change value or fail, and shortened the life of the tubes themselves.

While marked progress is being made in the dependability of electronic devices, much remains to be done to improve the reliability of home appliances. Dealers are quoted regularly in trade journals decrying the lack of quality control at the factory level. The prime headache appears to be refrigerators and air conditioners. Too many units are found to be dead on arrival and have to be either taken back or, if possible, repaired in the customer's home. This makes for an expensive unprofitable sale and a very tough public-relations problem.

The appliance dealers are smoldering over the manufacturer's alleged negligence in producing equipment with a burdensome degree of failure. The consumer must be doubly careful because, while a dealer may get singed, the consumer is the one who will get burned.

5

On Safari

To SET OUT to buy a specific make and model of an appliance or television set and actually come home with it requires more stamina and courage than a mountain climber. Many people wonder how they wound up with a Magnavox when they really thought they wanted a Zenith. Or is the Admiral really a better refrigerator than the General Electric they asked to see?

The reason this happens so frequently is that the customer has been "switched." In the appliance retailing business, a salesperson does not earn real money if he is merely an order taker. It is felt by management that any schoolboy or "ribbon clerk" can write an order for the advertised loss-leader or the unprofitable low-end model. It is the ability of a salesperson either to switch to more profitable brands or to sell up to higher-priced models that separates the men from the boys. The axiom in the retail appliance trade is that the salesman who sells the advertised models will find himself going along with the piece. Naturally, to make it worth a salesman's time and effort to improve the profit of a sale, some incentives have to be built into the merchandise he is supposed to push.

Federal and state wage-and-hour laws make it extremely costly to pay retail salesmen a guaranteed high

71

weekly salary plus commission. Most promotional stores find it expedient to pay a base salary which just covers the minimum hourly rate prescribed by law. Salesmen are then paid commissions varying from 1 to 5 percent or higher, depending upon the activity of the store and the amount of profit in the goods they sell. In a busy store a salesman is expected to be able to wait on enough customers so that in spite of a lower percentage of commissions, his weekly income will be sufficiently rewarding. In a less active store, a higher commission must be paid so that a salesman can make a living taking care of fewer customers.

In addition to a better commission on more profitable goods, salesmen are given "P.M.'s" (push money) or "spiffs." These are cash bonuses or rewards for selling the merchandise the store is most interested in moving. This merchandise again is made up of the more profitable lines, the last year's models, the "dogs" that just don't seem to get sold, or overstocked items.

Not only does the store hold out the carrot on the stick to the salesman, but the factories fight to buy the salesman's loyalty to their brands. The manufacturers are continually offering sales incentives to retail appliance salesmen. The kind of factory spiffs vary from Westinghouse's offering men's shirts for the sale of laundry equipment to Kelvinator's letting retail salesmen have a chance at a punch board for every refrigerator sold with prizes ranging from five to twenty dollars. The most prevalent practice is to pay cash bonuses in varying amounts directly to the salesman. Appliance factories do not generally have a year-round spiff program, and when they drop it a salesman's enthusiasm for that brand quickly dissolves.

A more subtle means of buying a salesman's dedication to a brand is employed with spectacular success by Magnavox. Magnavox places point values on every piece of merchandise in its line. Salesmen selling Magnavox products submit a list of their sales to the factory and are sent a certificate indicating the number of points they have earned. The prizes for which these points may be redeemed are depicted in a beautiful catalogue, which is sent directly to the salesman's home.

The Magnavox catalogue looks like a millionaire's S & H Green Stamp catalogue. Here the salesman's wife sees everything from mink stoles, diamond rings, cashmere sweaters, and alligator handbags to equally desirable furniture, linens and china, golf clubs, typewriters, cameras, skis, toys, and trips to Disneyland. The salesman wistfully realizes that he will have to sell a hell of a lot of Magnavox before the rest of the family will let him cash in his points for a new riding lawn mower, an outboard motor, or a belt sander for his workshop.

Sylvania has taken the cue from Magnavox and rewards retail salesmen with S & H Green Stamps for pushing their line. What these clever factory sales geniuses have done is to recruit a salesman's own family to promote the retail sales of their goods. The wife who is hoarding the points or stamps for a new living room rug won't give her hero a big kiss for selling a fancy Philco.

Naturally, in their schemes to engender loyalty and encourage sales effort behind each factory's product, the manufacturers do not neglect the store owners or buyers. Factories happily whisk the more important buyers to palatial hotels in exotic resorts like Nassau, Hawaii, Miami Beach, and Las Vegas whenever a new line is unveiled. There, in plush, almost sybaritic surroundings, the buyers from the Bronx, Cedar Rapids, and Biloxi are wined and dined and made to feel important. Away from the rat race and out from the steely eyes of controllers and merchandise managers, relaxed and docile buyers buy more than they had perhaps budgeted for.

As a matter of fact, the Hotpoint Division of General Electric got into a little difficulty with the Mann Act a few years ago when its New Jersey branch provided a more earthy type of entertainment for its better customers.

Following the national sales meetings attended by the factory distributors and representatives of the large retail accounts, the new models are shown to the lower caste of buyers at a local "dealer open house." These affairs are usually held either in the ballroom of the fanciest hotel available or at a local distributor's showroom if it has the facilities. Every dealer is welcome, from the department stores to the owners of the "mom and pop" stores, although nonbuyers like retail salesmen, servicemen, and wives are sometimes treated like lepers and considered freeloaders.

Regardless of whether the catering calls for a sitdown dinner or the more likely buffet of cold cuts and potato salad, the bar is always open. The dealer is taken in tow by his wholesale salesman, dragged past one model after another; then he is cornered and an order blank is shoved in front of him. How much sales resistance the buyer has at this point usually depends not so much on the merits of the product he has just seen, but on more subjective issues. These are the benefits included in the show "package" (extra emoluments to induce substantial orders at show time), the availability of sufficient "floor planning" (financing of goods by the manufacturer until they are sold), or the enticement of this year's "trip."

74

The appliance manufacturers and distributors have used with singular success the device of awarding a trip to some glamorous part of the world as a sales incentive to dealers. At one point a short time ago, before the Johnson administration made traveling outside North or South America seem unpatriotic, a good appliance dealer could get to see almost any popular tourist spot in the world.

Factories vied with one another to seek out more exotic places to take their dealers. Rome, Madrid, Paris, London, the Riviera, and Majorca had become mundane for the guys who could sell a lot of refrigerators and TV sets. New locales—Tel Aviv, Estoril, Athens, Vienna, Copenhagen, and even Hong Kong and Tokyo—were dangled before the dealers. An appliance-store owner or buyer is probably better traveled than his counterpart in any other retail business. Factories have flown thousands of dealers with their wives and point-earned movie cameras to almost every desirable resort or romantic capital city in the world. Sometimes ocean liners were chartered, in full or in part, for cruises to Bermuda, Nassau or Hawaii. Recently, places like Hawaii, Freeport, Acapulco, Aruba, and Puerto Rico have been very big. The real swinging factories branch out as far as Rio de Janeiro.

In order for a dealer to go along on one of these junkets, the trip must be "earned." He must purchase a prescribed amount of goods in order to qualify. Unless the dealer represents an outlet that has the capacity to sell large amounts of goods quickly, the purchase price of the quantities required to earn a trip is usually heavier than a dealer can normally absorb. There are appliance dealers who buy only for trips and others whose trip purchases have loaded them to the point where they could not turn the goods fast enough. They were choked to the point where to move trip merchandise they had to cut prices so much that they were selling at a loss and even jeopardized their ability to stay in business. It can be seen that the trip promotion is another pressure on dealers and salesmen to sell some merchandise in preference to others.

It should be borne in mind that all these retail sales incentives have their counterpart on the wholesale level. Salesmen working for manufacturers and distributors are prodded and rewarded with similar inducements. All of these promotions cost money, which has to be absorbed in the price the consumer pays and is just as much a part of nonmanufacturing overhead as TV or magazine advertising or quiz contest give-aways. Industry estimates of the cost of special buying incentives are currently about $150 million a year.

One other category of purchases that leads to certain appliances and television sets being pushed by stores and salesmen is the factory close-out. Large manufacturers naturally have in their inventories, from time to time, odds and ends of various models. These can be production overruns, discontinued models, cancellations, or a quantity of an item too small to bother to put into general distribution.

These close-outs are offered at important discounts to favored customers such as department stores, large chains, and buying groups. Sometimes, if the item is a real "dump," it may filter down to smaller dealers through regular distribution channels. In general, however, it is much more economical and politically expedient to reserve these goodies for individual large accounts than to peddle them piecemeal all over the country.

Close-outs are used as both a wedge and a club by factory sales managers; they are used to reward the loyal aggressive buyers and to entice new accounts into taking on a line. The recalcitrant or unenthusiastic account is punished by the factory's withholding from him a promotional model that his competition will use to beat the unfavored dealer's brains out.

A smart buyer will use all his talent and initiative to inveigle these close-outs from the manufacturer. The opportunities they offer for greater profits or more exciting promotions are extremely rewarding. There are some factories bright enough to recognize what a powerful sales tool close-outs represent. General Electric has had production lines busy making previous-year models of washing machines, refrigerators, and other appliances, which are offered to buyers, generally at prices lower than current models and too hot to pass up, when the market is soft or the sales of a particular distribution branch need a shot in the arm.

The type of merchandise offered as a close-out can range from the genuine buy to a marketing prognosticator's bad guess or a designer's flight of fancy. One thousand pink washing machines, refrigerators with various Formica fronts or all left-hand doors, radio-phonographs without stereo-FM, chocolate-colored dryers, and bilious Nile-green ranges are some of the goods that have taken the close-out route. Others have been freezers that were built like bank vaults, weighing as much as a small elephant and not even especially roomy inside.

The television industry has had its troubles trying to digest small-screen color TV consoles. These were the eighteen- and twenty-inch sets, which sell well as table models; but in wood-cabinet floor models priced close to the largest twenty-three-inch size, they were highly unsuccessful. When these sets were finally unloaded at a wholesale price realistic enough to move them out, alert buyers snapped them up. These were good color TV sets which could be offered to the public at up to a hundred dollars less than they were previously sold for and yet showed a better-than-average profit for the retailer. Motorola and Sylvania had the worst cases of twenty-inch color console indigestion, with other companies suffering in milder degree.

How tough can a customer be when shopping for a new appliance or TV set? In order to buy what he wants he has to be able to resist a persuasive pitch from a highly motivated salesman and a carefully planned attack on his sales resistance. The customer is up against an adversary hungry for spiffs and extra commissions busily doing the mental arithmetic involved in counting points and Green Stamps. The store itself is set up so that the high markup lines, the goods that were overbought, the "trip" merchandise and the close-outs get the maximum exposure.

What tactics are employed by stores and their sales people in order to change a buyer's mind and sell what they are most anxious to move? The first requirement of retailing is a carnival-borrowed slogan, "You have to get the sucker under the tent."

Advertising performs this function. In order to attract the greatest number of "bodies," this advertising has to offer what seem like fantastic bargains and impart some urgency to them. "Six-hour Sales," "Moonlight Madness," "Krazy Daze," "Saturday Only," and holiday promotions like "Washington's Birthday Sale" are all efforts in this vein.

When a shopper comes into a store and asks to see

an item that was advertised at a patently ridiculous price, he becomes the victim of the "bait and switch" operation. The customer has been led into the "tent" seeking the advertised special, and now it is the salesman's function to sell him something else. Sometimes there is no sample ("We're all sold out!"), or the sample, when it is available, is so unappetizing as to border on the revolting. Wringer washers are shown with dirty gray outer tubs, or freezers have black inner food-compartment liners. Prospects for the advertised automatic washer are told that the bargain model has only a single fill hose and can't regulate the water temperature. Vegetable crisper drawers and shelves are removed from refrigerators, but made available in the next higher priced models. Or the "ADV" (advertised special) refrigerator is available only with the less frequently desired left-hand door.

At one time it was common practice to remove one antenna lead from the terminals inside the back of advertised or short markup television sets so that their pictures would suffer by comparison with the makes a store was really pushing. This dodge finally led Zenith and other TV makers to mount the tuner leads on the outside of the cabinet back, where anyone can see if the set is properly hooked up. Refrigerators touted as "family-sized" turn out to be suitable for a pair of "Munchkins" and "giant-sized" television screens are sometimes little larger than knotholes.

The term "naildown" is used in the trade to describe the loss-leaders and hot specials that are employed as bait and are never sold. Some stores will keep the ninety-nine-dollar Maytag wringer washer with the mottled gray tub or the repossessed round-screen color TV set on their floors for years. Manufacturers will make models that are intended to be naildowns. These are the television cabinets in sickly green or morbid black from which one would normally recoil unless he wanted to build it into a storage wall. Washers are made lacking lint filters, water-level settings, water-temperature or speed controls. Dryers with one low-wattage fixed heat, devoid of any vestige of aesthetic appeal, also fall into the nail-down category.

When the "special" is rejected by the customer or he is told that it will be unavailable for an indefinite period, he is then waltzed over to a really deluxe, top-of-the-line, high-priced model. All of its features are rhapsodized by the salesman. If the prospect is intrigued, but murmurs, "It's too much money," he is then taken to the "sell" model. This is the model that the store really intended to sell when it advertised the nail-down. The customer is shown that it has practically all the features of the expensive model and, except for the lack of a few conveniences and trim items, will do the same job. "Anyway," the salesman confidentially asks the prospect, "who wants to pay extra for all that gingerbread?"

If the sale has not been made at this point, or the salesman feels that the customer is about to "walk," the "TO" man is brought in. "TO" stands for "turn over" or "take over." The TO man may be the store manager, an owner, or merely another salesman who is introduced to the customer as someone in a supervisory position. Stores employing the TO system feel that if the first salesman has not been able to close the sale in a reasonable length of time it may be due to a personality conflict between the salesman and the customer. The TO man introduces a fresh personality into the proceedings and is a further assault on the customer's resistance. The TO man has to be a strong closer, and able to brush aside objections to the product, give reasons as to value and performance, and promote confidence. Since the practice of using TO men occurs mainly in stores without a firm price, the TO man must also be a skilled negotiator. Some really hard-sell stores will throw two or even three TO men at a customer before he either buys or manages to escape.

Many appliance stores operate without exposed prices. Price tags are coded alphabetically or use a reverse numerical sequence. Sometimes high fictitious list prices are shown so that the price asked seems like a substantial discount or the price tag advises the customer to ask the salesman for the "discount" price. Stores will defend the practice of concealing or omitting actual selling prices on two grounds. They claim that they do not want to make it easy for competitors to shop them out, or that the manufacturers will get sore at them for selling too low. Both of these arguments, while plausible, are not factual.

The real reason for concealing or otherwise confusing the prices is that there is no true selling price. The codes represent the lowest price the store will take for a particular appliance or television set. Above that amount, it is up to the salesman to get what the traffic will bear. He may earn a substantial portion of his income from his participation in the "OC," or "overcharge," which is what this pernicious practice is called. It is possible for a store to sell a dozen pieces of the same item without two customers paying the same price. A store can justify the OC to itself by calculating that even if it gives the salesman 25 percent or more of the additional charge, the customer is really paying the salesman's entire salary and commission with the extra profit. Naturally, it is the less-informed, poorer-educated consumer or the marginal credit risk who is most often "lumped" in this manner.

The cynical advertising, sales, and merchandising methods outlined here are not to be construed as universally prevalent in the appliance and television business. While many stores operate in a highly ethical and fair manner, others will resort to some or all of the practices described. Whether it is a small neighborhood dealer, a merchandising giant operating hundreds of big retail outlets, or a mail-order or catalogue store, a careful buyer should be alert to the ingenious but unscrupulous schemes that are employed to his disadvantage.

6

My Guarantee Says . . .

THE GUARANTEE on a new appliance or television set is supposed to give a new owner the same sense of security as a child's fuzzy blanket. Snuggled up in the comfort of the legal language on the engraved certificate, he feels that someone is going to take care of him with kindness and love. The awakening comes when a buyer has trouble, asks for help, and discovers he is an orphan.

No aspect of the appliance industry has brought so much attention to itself as the manufacturers' and dealers' failure to live up to the warranties upon which the merchandise was sold. Congressmen are receiving complaints from constituents who have been unable to get service difficulties or product malfunctions attended to. The federal government's avowed dedication to the plight of the consumer makes for a popular crusade and doesn't cost too much money. It is undeniably politically attractive to champion the cause of the helpless citizen against the power of organized big business. The appointment of Betty Furness as watchdog and spokesman for the consumer's interests was a brilliant and popular maneuver. Miss Furness was associated in the public's mind with consumer products from her exposure on television as a soft-sell saleslady of home appliances.

Her campaign for the consumer, while not of the muckraking kind, nevertheless developed a fair amount of momentum. Her efforts were well directed and timely and made good newspaper copy. The grass-roots support her programs developed has already borne legislative results. The passage of a truth-in-lending law by the Congress is attributable in large measure to the attention she focused on the abuses in the lending of money or financing of consumer goods. This bill languished in Congress for eight years until the climate of concern for consumer problems forced its passage.

Next Miss Furness took up the cudgel for the consumer in the battle to strengthen warranties and ensure the fulfillment of the manufacturer's promises. This is what has brought the congressmen the mail reflecting some of the frustration that was formerly directed to the factories. The fact that congressmen are sensitive to such an appeal has not been lost on the manufacturers.

Meetings, conferences, symposiums, and just plain "bull sessions" are being held by industry groups such as the National Association of Manufacturers, the Association of Home Appliance Manufacturers, the American Gas Association, and the Electronics Industries Association. Even the American Retail Federation, whose members include Sears, Montgomery Ward, and J. C. Penney, has met to discuss the implications of the new awareness of the weakness of warranties. The government and large retail interests hope to be able to persuade the manufacturers to come up with an acceptable form of product warranty. The manufacturers, however, don't need the retailers to remind them of the urgency of the situation. They are scurrying around trying to find a formula that will forestall the threatened legislation. Speaking before the convention of the Gas Appliance Manufacturers Association, Truman B. Clark of the Tappan Company and the association's Chairman of Consumer Affairs, made this statement as reported in the April 28, 1969, edition of *Home Furnishings Daily:* "I'm afraid if we do not show them [the government] we are doing something, then the next step is possible legislation and you know we will get something that will be hard to digest."

Trying to develop a uniform, fully disclosive form of guarantee or warranty that the average buyer can decipher is an uncomfortable task. It is complicated by the specter of the government threatening antitrust action if the manufacturers actually put their heads together and come up with a cut-and-dried warranty form that would become standard for the industry.

One of the questions most frequently asked by customers shopping for an appliance is, "Is it guaranteed?" They are assured that it certainly is and are shown an impressive-looking document that accompanies the product. Their confidence in this piece of paper is enough to overcome any fears they may have concerning the performance or durability of the product, and the sale can usually be closed right at this point.

This warranty in which the buyer has placed so much trust has been proved all too frequently to be a weak vessel. A customer understands a product warranty to be a contract or surety that if he has trouble, it will be taken care of. He does not expect to pay for labor, parts, or damage to his property due to product malfunction during the period of time the warranty is in force. It is regarded in the same way as an all-risk insurance policy on his house or car and he expects to have it cover all minor eventualities or major catastrophes without any deductibles.

However, the bare bones of the usual appliance warranty are quite different. All the manufacturer takes it upon himself to do is repair or replace any parts that are proven within a given period of time to be defective in either workmanship or material. The questions of how the parts are discovered to be faulty or who will return them, freight prepaid, to the factory, or who will install the replaced parts, are left in limbo.

It is generally assumed that it is the obligation of the seller to perform the labor associated with the repairs of an appliance. No such assumption is entirely valid. A dealer has no contractual obligation to perform service on in-warranty appliances, but the fact is that he does or contracts with others to do this at his expense. The reason he has been providing no-charge service all this time is that the factories have either seduced or bullied him into believing that he must. That the factories have been able to perpetuate this inequity does little credit to the intelligence of appliance dealers.

The same factories that pay their new-car dealers to service Chevrolets, Fords, and Ramblers for up to two years, expect Frigidaire, Philco, or Kelvinator dealers to perform this service for nothing, or charge him if they do it for him. As long as manufacturers can worry only about pumping the product out of their factories and leave it to the dealers and service companies to rectify their mistakes, appliance warranties will have little meaning to the consumer.

Speaking to a group of dealers and manufacturers at the New York City meeting of the Electronics Industries Association, Paul Dixon, then Federal Trade Commission chairman, complained that most warranties cover parts only and tend to limit the liability of the manufacturers.

He is quoted in the June 17, 1969, issue of *Consumer Electronics* as follows:

"I think it's pretty clear that the manufacturers and sellers of products must be prepared to give more extensive warranties than they have in the past."

Legislation may not be required to accomplish this objective, the FTC chief said—although it is a strong possibility—since the doctrine of "implied warranty" holds the manufacturer responsible for the performance of merchandise sold. "The law says you sell me a television set, and whether it's one year or 10 years it better have a picture on it—and if it's your fault, you'd better make it good.

"We receive complaint after complaint about color television sets being delivered in defective condition, followed by reluctance of dealers and manufacturers to repair them. The plain fact appears to be that industry is not willing to bear the expense of correcting its mistakes and has attempted to shift the cost of doing so to the consumer."

The most ludicrous, yet sad, comment made by the customer unhappy about the failure of a new appliance is, "Why don't you take it back? The factory will make good on it." This is said to the dealer who sold it and who knows that the factory couldn't care less. If he exchanges it, he eats it. Rarely will a factory take back, replace, or otherwise pay for an appliance which proved to be defective on delivery. Even a DOA (dead on arrival) refrigerator must be carted out of a customer's house, replaced with a new one, and then be repaired at the dealer's expense.

Only when a dealer represents an extremely strong retail outlet does he get any real help from his suppliers.

Otherwise, he has to foot all the repair, trucking, and bookkeeping bills and wind up with a used piece of equipment that he cannot sell at a profit.

In the fight to maintain a competitive edge in the market, manufacturers are now offering extended parts warranties. When a company moves to lengthen the warranty on all laundry equipment parts from one to two years, the others quickly follow suit. Frigidaire created a flurry by offering a five-year warranty on certain specific parts in other appliances besides washers and dryers. These extended parts warranties are more of a sales-promotion gimmick than any real evidence that the product is being made better. They are supposed to reinforce the consumer's confidence in a brand by suggesting that the product must be good if the factory is willing to stand behind it all that time.

The real effect is to put a further burden on the dealer or service agency, who must go through the expensive rigmarole of returning in-warranty parts for credit. The manufacturer has not incurred a great deal of extra risk, as the parts most likely to fail—timers, solenoids, heating elements, valves, and switches—can be returned to the vendors who supplied them. Parts made by the prime manufacturers—cabinets, tubs, liners, and other structural parts—either do not normally fail or are not covered by the extended warranty.

Extended warranties on other parts of home appliances also tend to be misleading. Every purchaser of a refrigerator, home freezer, or room air conditioner is given to understand that everything in it is guaranteed (parts and labor) for a period of one year. This is what the salesman recites when he is selling the product. He will also tell the buyer that the compressor, the real heart of a piece of refrigeration equipment, is guaranteed for five years.

This isn't the way the manufacturer understands or writes his warranty. At no time does he guarantee against defective light bulbs, breakage of plastic or porcelain parts, or leakage of refrigerant gas. This means that even during the first year's operation, if a plastic shelf or bracket should break, the porcelain craze, or the refrigerant seep out of a pinhole leak or poorly soldered connection, the manufacturer accepts no responsibility. How well the buyer can get these problems attended to will depend upon the integrity and generosity of the dealer who sold it. Factory-operated or factory-authorized service agencies generally tend to adhere to a strict interpretation of the language in the warranty. Owners will find themselves charged for repairs during the warranty period that can be the fault of poor design or fabrication.

When a refrigerator compressor fails within the first five years, the factory will replace it. The customer is not reimbursed for the inconvenience, aggravation, and delay. Rarely can a new compressor be installed in less than a week. First, you must get the serviceman to come and look at it. During a hot spell, when most compressors give up, this is not easy. When the repairman does arrive, he says, "I'll have to order out a new one." This can take several days, the length of time depending on the distance from the parts depot. The actual replacement of the compressor in a customer's home can tie up the kitchen for hours, with the serviceman working with pumps, gas tanks, gauges, and torches. If the compressor breaks down after the expiration date of the warranty, throw the refrigerator away; it is cheaper to buy a new one.

When food is spoiled and has to be thrown away due to a refrigeration breakdown within the guarantee period, who pays for it? That's easy. You do. Except in the case of home freezers and a few Duplex-style refrigerators with large freezer sections, the customer is never reimbursed for a nickel's worth of lost food. Most home freezers and a few of the Duplexes do have a policy against food spoilage that is underwritten by major insurance companies. In order to collect on it, the customer must make a sworn statement as to the contents of the freezer and their value. The nature of the failure and how it was repaired must be attested to by the servicing agency in the form of a notarized affidavit. The manufacturers and insurance companies do not make it easy, but at least there is some protection there.

A similar rude awakening awaits the automatic-washer owner whose machine needs transmission repairs. Like the compressor in a refrigerator, this is the most costly component in a washer and is also warranted for five years. You will get the replacement transmission or the parts needed to fix it, but you will also get a service charge that may make it seem as though you were buying the machine all over again.

Home electronic equipment, such as radios, portable phonographs, tape recorders, and some portable television sets, generally carry a ninety-day parts warranty. All color television, some black-and-white TV, and most large console stereo sets have a one-year warranty on parts. Free labor is furnished for only ninety days. The means by which a consumer can obtain this free service are somewhat nebulous and inconsistent. All portable television sets, portable stereos, radios, and tape recorders have to be brought or shipped to either a servicing dealer or an authorized repair agency. There they will be repaired free of charge to the owner. Larger units—color television sets, console black-and-white television sets, and console stereos—require in-home servicing. Manufacturers make no provision for this unless the set was sold with an added service charge, which is tacked on to or included in the purchase price. In general, the manufacturer accepts no responsibility for the labor during the ninety-day warranty period and leaves it up to the dealer to make any needed repairs. Regardless of any claims the TV manufacturers may make about screening their retail outlets to make sure they are able to render competent service, they are more interested in sales performance. As I pointed out earlier, factory franchises are revoked more often because of poor sales rather than an inability to service.

The picture tube in a color television set is a very costly item. Standard practice for the industry was to warrant this part for one year. If it failed during the first ninety days of service it was replaced free of charge to the customer, with the dealer paying for the labor. After ninety days, but within the one-year period, the tube is still free of charge but the customer has to pay for the labor of replacing it. The charge for this service will range from $25 to $50, and the technician who does the work conscientiously is entitled to the higher figure. A customer whose color picture tube failed after the one-year period was faced with a replacement tube cost of between $125 and $175, plus the cost of labor. This could come about when a set bought on time payments was less than half paid for.

A rising incidence of color picture tube failures after the warranty period expired and the consequent outcry from unlucky set owners caused the television manufacturers to extend their color picture tube warranties to two years. Admiral is presently offering a three-year color

93

tube warranty, using the extra year as a crutch in aid of sales. The manufacturers have not been carried away by their generosity, however. In order to cover their exposure on the second-year warranty, they have charged the dealers an extra $7.50 on each set in their stock as of the date the warranty was extended. They have suggested to the dealer that he either absorb it or pass it on to the customer. The period during which the labor is free to the customer is still only ninety days.

The factories still refuse to underwrite any part of the labor costs involved in changing faulty in-warranty color television tubes. This is perhaps the most unfair hardship that a dealer or consumer is subject to under the terms of any warranty. A color picture tube fails because it was made improperly. There is very little a set owner can do to make it go bad.

The manufacture of color tubes calls for the utmost precision in the fabrication of its parts, in assembly, and in testing. The high price of color television is a reflection of the fact that the cost of building these tubes to critical standards has been figured into the selling price. There is no moral or ethical justification for penalizing the dealer or the consumer when the tubes fail to deliver the life or performance their high cost would lead one to expect.

When the sales of color television began to boom in 1965 there were only three manufacturers with enough color tube production to meet the demand. These three were RCA, Sylvania, and National Video, who was Motorola's main supplier. They supplied the other set manufacturers who had just begun pilot production on their own tubes or whose tube factories were still on the drawing boards. As sales snowballed it quickly became apparent that RCA, Sylvania, and National Video would have difficulty supplying tubes for their own sets. The manufacturers who bought from them were placed on a rationing of tubes, which curtailed their production and lost them sales. Under these circumstances, Philco, General Electric, Zenith, Admiral, and Westinghouse rushed to get color tube production from their own plants.

The manufacture of color picture tubes is an extremely demanding technical process. Because of the seemingly inexhaustible demand for sets, tubes were turned out before the plants making them were fully experienced. An example of this was the Rauland tube division of Zenith. Like the rest of the TV makers in 1965, Zenith was caught by the tube shortage and pushed Rauland into production of the relatively new twenty-three-inch rectangular tube. In spite of a lack of proper quality control and technical know-how, the tubes were just shipped because the cabinets and chassis were waiting; and Zenith tubes failed at an alarming rate. Some dealers had to replace tubes in as many as 25 percent of their new Zenith color television sets. Since Zenith couldn't make the tubes fast enough for its production lines, replacement tubes were hard to get. Customers sometimes had to wait several weeks to be able to enjoy a brand-new color television set for which they might have already paid. Sets in dealers' stocks lay useless and unsalable, tying up space and money.

Zenith eventually replaced all the defective tubes, but no one was reimbursed for the labor of reinstalling the tubes and the freight in handling them. The consumer and the dealers in effect bore part of the cost of debugging and shaking down a new product and plant.

The manufacturers are not concerned about the burdens the implementing of warranties places upon the dealer. Performing service functions or correcting factory mistakes raises a dealer's cost of doing business and shortens already precarious profit margins. This further prejudices his capacity to cope with the responsibilities an appliance warranty unloads upon him. In essence, the manufacturer's warranty says, "Complain to the guy you bought it from. We don't want to be bothered."

The attitude of the industry toward the warranty and service problem as it affects the consumer is reflected in a statement made by Guenther Baumgart, president of the Association of Home Appliance Manufacturers, and quoted in the July 15, 1968, issue of *Home Furnishings Daily:* "One possible way to alleviate the service problem is to make the consumers aware that their appliance budgets should cover the cost of initial investment, service, and replacement."

Has Mr. Baumgart made that statement to the poor soul whose color picture tube went out thirteen months after he bought the set and who will still be paying $32.50 a month for twenty-three more months?

7

Straight from the
Factory to You

IT IS WORTH following the route an appliance travels in its journey from the factory to the home of the customer. The distribution system of the appliance industry is a study of methods that are sometimes inefficient and quite often costly.

Factories most often use a two-step method of distribution whereby the goods are sold to a regional distributor, who in turn sells them to a retailer. The advantage for the manufacturer is that the distributor is responsible for selling a predetermined amount of product in his market. A manufacturer will decide that a particular distributor's territory should represent a certain proportion of his company's production. For instance, the New York City area is usually thought to be a 10 to 12 percent market, while the entire state of Connecticut would be only a 2 percent market. This means that the New York distributor has to be counted upon to sell around 10 percent of factory output while the Connecticut distributor should use around 2 percent.

In the case of a company whose line has good national acceptance and high productive capacity, the demands upon the distributors can be rigorous. Any distributor who fails to sell what the factory thinks his market area should absorb soon finds the franchise lifted and given to someone else. By allocating responsibility for the coverage of all marketing areas to independent distribution companies, the factories have a fair idea of where the goods are going before they are produced. At the time when a new line is shown to distributors, the factory, if it is in a strong market position, hands the distributor a commitment for the merchandise he is expected to buy for, say, the next six months. Distributors who value their franchise are not inclined to haggle at this point, and so they just sign what amounts to a blank order.

Now the manufacturer knows what he is going to produce, where it is going, and who is going to pay for it. He doesn't have to worry about peddling it to ten or twenty thousand individual outlets or setting up the credit, collection, warehousing, and shipping facilities to service that many separate accounts. The factory just wheels the merchandise into solid freight cars and out it goes. The burden of disposing of it is off their shoulders.

When business is good and the line proves to be hot, or the demand for the product is greater than the supply —as was the case with color television a few years ago— the distributor is sitting pretty. He has something everybody wants, he's the only place they can get it, and the prices he charges his dealer customers provide him with a very handsome profit.

When a line is doing well the distributor is happy to be selling it and to assume his usual risks. The distributor's function is to maintain a sales staff to promote the sale of the brands he represents to the best retail outlets he can secure. He must be strong enough financially to store in his own warehouse the large inventories that the factories insist upon, and he must be able to carry considerable accounts receivable from his dealers. He is also expected to maintain a service department to provide information and assistance on technical problems and act as a depot for replacement parts.

These operations are costly, and the distributor must price the lines he is wholesaling high enough to cover his overhead and provide a profit. They also add substantially to the ultimate price that has to be charged the consumer.

The manufacturers are aware of the profits to be made at the distribution end of the business. Each year their independent distributors must furnish them with a financial statement. The factories require these statements so that they may be sure their distributors are fiscally sound enough to pay for the goods they are shipped.

After a few years of studying the profits made by distributors as shown in their successive statements, the factories realized that there was just as much money to be made in distribution as in manufacturing. One by one, independent distributors in the lusher markets have had their franchises revoked and their operations turned over to factory-controlled distribution branches.

A case in point is the Chase Electric Company of New Haven, Connecticut, which had been an independent distributor of Westinghouse major appliances for twenty-five years. Its territory comprised the state of Connecticut and western Massachusetts. Each year it was at or near the top of the list of Westinghouse distributors, both factory and independent. This list is based on what is known as percentage of industry and market penetration; that is, the share of goods Westinghouse sold in that market as compared to other competing brands.

Chase Electric was a father-and-son business and operated on the highest ethical principles. Chase's dealers knew that if they had a problem with a defective piece of Westinghouse merchandise, Chase would solve it. The people who worked for Chase Electric were also outstanding and were extremely well paid. The credit, sales, and service managers, and even the people in charge of locating merchandise and expediting orders, were genuinely interested in helping their dealers. Extended terms for payment were worked out when a dealer was short of funds, and Bob Chase even went so far as to personally endorse notes for dealers at their own banks.

The salesmen who called on the Westinghouse dealers served by Chase Electric were also top professionals. They were chosen more for qualities of honesty and helpfulness than for superior sales ability. Chase never paid these men a commission because he felt that they might then be tempted to sell a customer more than he really needed. Yet he always had a waiting list of people anxious to represent him, as he paid his men a very comfortable salary and furnished them with a new car every year.

By doing business in this highly ethical fashion for twenty-five years, the Chase Electric organization built up an almost fanatical loyalty among its dealers. If a dealer carried more than one line, Westinghouse would always get preference in terms of representation and promotional effort. On the other hand, if Chase Electric had a problem with an overstock of a particular model it could go to its dealers and ask for help, and the dealers would place orders to get the distributor off the hook.

In September 1964, the Westinghouse Corporation informed Chase Electric Company that its franchise would not be renewed after December 31 and that the territory would be taken over by the Westinghouse Appliance Sales Company, a factory branch. The reaction of Chase's dealers was gloom and indignation. Practically every Chase customer fired off a telegram or letter to Donald Burnham, then the president of the Westinghouse Electric Company. The messages begged Westinghouse to reconsider its action, and some dealers threatened to discontinue handling the line altogether.

Mr. Burnham answered all the letters politely and uniformly, stating that he recognized Chase's outstanding record and sympathized with the loyalty of his dealers. However, "developments in marketing and future planning" necessitated this action.

Westinghouse could see from Chase's financial statements that it was running a high-cost distributorship. Besides paying personnel far more than the going rate and operating a costly service department, Bob Chase, the president of the company, was drawing a very substantial salary. In spite of these unusual expenses the company showed a respectable profit, and the net assets of the company continued to increase.

It did not require any CPA genius at Westinghouse to figure that by taking over Chase's distributorship the factory could make even more money than Chase. By budgeting personnel and operating at a normal level and eliminating an owner's salary, Westinghouse could come up with spectacular operating economies. From this, it could be expected that Westinghouse should be able to sell its product in the Connecticut market more cheaply. This would be an economically desirable outcome and would justify the cold-blooded take-over of a sound, respected, family-owned business.

This was not the case. Prices charged to dealers were not reduced. Without the flexibility of a locally owned business, the factory branch had to hew the line marked out for it by headquarters. From time to time Bob Chase had made special purchases available to his dealers of a refrigerator or a television set that he was able to pick up from the factory. He would fly out to a plant, find out what it wanted to unload, make an offer, and buy on the spot. However, with the take-over of his franchise, the opportunity for small dealers to pick up these goodies and make a little extra profit or create an exciting promotion just about dried up.

What happened to Chase Electric has been happening to independent distributors all over the country. In the past ten or fifteen years General Electric, Frigidaire, RCA, Zenith, Philco-Ford, Whirlpool, and other giants have gobbled up the franchises of independently owned distributors. The few remaining privately owned distributors for the major lines are now located in territories so remote or thinly populated that the factories would just as soon leave the independents to scratch out a living in these markets.

The record has not shown that running a presumably more efficient operation has lowered the cost to the retailer and ultimately to the consumer. All that has happened is that the dealer is deprived of a source of supply that could be sympathetic to his troubles, help him in running his business, and be interested in keeping him as a sound and growing customer.

After five years of controlling practically all of the distribution of Westinghouse appliances, the factory has found that that end of the business is not all roses. While it was nice making both the distribution and the manufacturing profit, it has, in some areas, suffered a loss in percentage of market. It has closed up factory branches covering markets like Buffalo, New York; Harrisburg, Pennsylvania; Portland, Maine; Montana; and parts of

Ohio and Washington state. The local distributors Westinghouse has franchised are rich, well-entrenched companies who have been successfully distributing RCA and Zenith. Now that Westinghouse has gone out of the television and console stereo business it does not compete with the profitable RCA and Zenith lines, which the new distributors would have been reluctant to abandon.

Westinghouse has come to realize that the independent distributor who knows his market and has easy access to dealers because of the desirability of his electronics line is better able to get the coverage in these territories. While it has not abandoned factory-owned distribution branches altogether, Westinghouse is now studying its marketing setup with a more flexible attitude. R. L. Sargent, a Westinghouse vice-president, has been quoted in the trade press as saying that Westinghouse is studying its marketing operation and will contemplate changes only where it feels that the independent distribution would do a better job than a factory branch.

Having tasted the profits of the distribution aspect of the business, the factories next cast greedy eyes on the retailing end. Here, they reasoned, is another inefficient, costly method of distribution that is also capable of making a profit. General Electric has opened a number of retail stores in Ohio and upper New York state. These outlets, while ostensibly owned and operated by private individuals, are really captive company stores.

All of the identification in signs and advertising stresses the General Electric logo. General Electric locates the sites, negotiates the leases, designs the signs, storefronts, and interior layouts. It also provides the financing of the merchandise and the customer's time payments through the General Electric Credit Corporation, a finance-company subsidiary. Furthermore, only General Electric merchandise is sold, from toasters to television sets. All of the advertising, sales training, and servicing is handled by General Electric, and the company will also deliver all sold goods to the consumer from its central warehouse.

General Electric finds a man with a little money to invest to run these push-button stores, and then puts him in business. It is just as much a franchise operation as Carvel Ice Cream or Colonel Sanders' Kentucky Fried Chicken.

Westinghouse has tried this type of store in Columbus, Ohio, and Charlotte, North Carolina, without even bothering to find a private owner to use as a straw man. Only the fear of massive antitrust action on the part of the United States Justice Department is curbing the manufacturers from making a more aggressive move into retail sales. Were it not for this restraint, the appliance companies could envision a beautiful vertical operation —right from producing a finished product to delivering it to the consumer's home.

Magnavox and a few other electronics producers have another method of distribution. They use no intermediate distributor, either independent or factory-owned. Salesmen, controlled directly by the factory's sales division, call directly on dealers and take orders, which are shipped from regional warehouses located around the country. Magnavox even ships most orders in its own trucks.

The savings accrued by this direct factory-to-dealer distribution are reflected in somewhat better retail markups. The retail prices are fixed by Magnavox through fair-trade laws where they exist and by tacit agreement where they don't. A Magnavox dealer can expect a better profit on this line than on one he has to purchase from a distributor. However, the price the consumer pays is not much, if any, less than he would pay for comparable models of RCA or Zenith. The difference saved between distributing Magnavox and distributing its competition is shared by the dealers and Magnavox. This tends to make Magnavox more profitable to sell, and consequently dealers put their strongest sales efforts behind it.

Independent appliance dealers had long been aware that their department and chain store competitors enjoyed more favorable buying arrangements than they did. Being able to use larger quantities of merchandise, the chains could pressure factories and distributors for the most favorable deals and terms. Preferential deals were made giving these big outlets extra advertising funds, special "in-store" merchandising allowances, and first crack at close-outs and "derivative" models. A "derivative" or "variation" model is one on which a piece of trim or a shelf is changed on a refrigerator, or a different color is used on a washer or range backguard. The item is given a model number not found in the regular line, and its distribution is confined to one major account in each market. When a store has an "exclusive" model, its price cannot be effectively comparison shopped. The biggest advantage of all was sheer buying power.

In order to comply with the Robinson-Patman Act, the manufacturers have to make the same deal available to all their customers. To overcome this obstacle and still favor the larger outlets, they set up a program of volume-incentive rebates: the more an account buys, the higher the percentage of rebate on its total purchases. General Electric sets up a quota in units, while Westinghouse computes its rebates on the basis of dollar volume. The larger the purchases, the more sizable the rebates, which range from ½ percent to 6 percent or more.

This situation brought about the emergence of cooperative appliance-buying groups as an important marketing force. The independent retailers, realizing that they could not compete as individuals, formed associations to pool as much of their buying power as possible. Dealers located in a marketing area that could be served by a central warehouse banded together and invested as much as twenty-five thousand dollars each. With this money a nonprofit corporation was formed and offices and warehouses set up.

Purchases could now be made in huge quantities when the requirements of all the members were taken into consideration. Suddenly, merchandise, special prices, and deals became available that these dealers never dreamed existed. Wherever possible, purchases were negotiated directly with factories in an effort to bypass the distributors and buy the merchandise at or below the distributor costs. These groups made every effort to buy at the best possible prices. Frills such as trips, cooperative advertising, salesmen's "spiffs" and any other promotional allowance were wrung out of the price. Coop members, who for years had been buying from the distributor "sheet," woke up to find that the prices they were now paying had improved on the average by about 10 percent.

The way these cooperative buying groups work can best be illustrated by giving a brief history of MARTA Co-operative, Inc., presently the largest such appliance-buying coop. MARTA was born in 1949 when a manufacturer's invoice intended for VIM Stores wound up at Bressner's TV in Brooklyn, New York. Bressner's, then a relatively small appliance chain, recognized that the prices being charged to VIM were considerably less than Bressner's was paying. When Bressner's questioned the supplier, it was told that VIM's much greater volume accounted for the difference.

The principals of Bressner's got on the phone and rounded up a few other Brooklyn dealers, some of whom were even competitors. The group formed a corporation with an initial investment of fifteen thousand dollars per dealer. In a short time a New Jersey chapter was formed, and in 1960 affiliated MARTA groups were organized in Connecticut, Philadelphia, and Washington, D.C. Later on, affiliated chapters were started in the Middle West.

Each local group is separately incorporated, maintains its own warehouse and has its own officers. All of the billing, inventory control, control of members' credit lines, retrieval of advertising funds, and payments for purchases is handled in MARTA's hundred-thousand-square-foot offices and central warehouse in Garden City, Long Island. There an office staff of over fifty people, working with elaborate data processing equipment, handles annual purchases of close to $100 million.

For years, MARTA had no paid officers. Officers are elected from among the members and serve without pay. Members are assigned as buyers for individual lines and are responsible for keeping an adequate supply of merchandise on hand at all times. Also, each buyer has to make sure of proper turnover so that merchandise does not languish in the warehouse and become superseded by new models. It is the duty of a buyer to learn as much as he can about the brand that he buys. He must be constantly in touch with the supplier and dealers in other markets to know what the best deals are.

At the weekly meetings held by each local chapter,

the buyers report on the movement of their lines out of the warehouse and the status of the goods ordered or en route, and discuss further buying commitments in each line MARTA handles.

Members of the group, who are generally the owners of the retail appliance stores which make up the co-operative, feel that the time they spend away from their stores on MARTA business is well spent. Information is exchanged at meetings which can make members quickly aware of changes in the industry. A member who runs a successful promotion is expected to share the news with his colleagues.

Since MARTA operates under the laws governing co-operatives and cannot show a profit, dealers are charged exactly what MARTA pays for the goods. The expense of running the huge New York office is split up among the members according to a simple formula. Half of the expense is shared equally among all members, and the other half is shared according to the volume of each member's purchases. These charges will add from as much as 5 percent or more to a smaller dealer's costs to as little as 1½ percent to a member whose monthly volume exceeds a hundred thousand dollars.

MARTA and similar appliance-buying cooperatives have had an important impact on the suppliers in markets where they are active. Distributors are unhappy either because they are being circumvented by the groups' ability to make direct factory deals or because they have to sell to a group at considerably less than normal profit.

A factory sales manager once complained that MARTA was trying to squeeze more out of his company's price than he was able to give. The president and one of the founders of MARTA, Bernard Artz, replied, "We don't want any special deals. Just treat us like you would Sears, Roebuck!"

It is not the intention of appliance-buying coops such as MARTA to pass their buying advantage along to the retail customer. These dealers have struggled a long time in a business where gross markups of 15 percent were common. Now, when their purchasing power and shift to more profitable lines have moved the markup to 25 percent or better, they are not about to give it away. The slogan repeated over and over within the buying group is, "The name of the game is *profit!*" As a sidelight on this theme, MARTA uses an alphabetical code to quote prices in the weekly bulletin sent to members. The code is:

MAKE PROFIT
1 2 3 4 5 6 7 8 9 0

Aside from the obvious desire to retain the extra profit margins from group purchasing in their own businesses, there are other strong reasons for these stores not to bombard their competition with outrageously low prices. MARTA feels that its member stores should be strong enough, and so well merchandised with the diverse lines that MARTA handles, that they can dominate their markets without resorting to indiscriminate and unprofitable price cutting.

Also, they refrain from advertising retail prices that are lower or sometimes only slightly above what their nongroup competitors are paying wholesale. Arousing the small dealers to ask their suppliers how MARTA members can sell an item at a retail below regular wholesale can make too many waves. Manufacturers and distributors are very sensitive to any rumblings that might cause a charge of price discrimination, bring on Federal Trade

Commission investigation, or engender unfavorable publicity in the trade or public press. Rather than run those risks, a manufacturer will cancel the group's program and will sell to them only on a no-advantage basis.

A buying-group member who willfully upsets his market by advertising prices on a particular brand substantially below the market can cause his group to blow the deal. The penalty for this, at least within MARTA, is quite severe. A member who causes the entire group to lose a line or buying advantage is fined one thousand dollars for a first offense. Subsequent infractions may bring expulsion from the group.

While the long-range trend of retail appliance stores is to form into cooperative buying organizations to improve their competitive position and profit margins, it is not expected that the consumer will benefit from lower prices.

There is in the appliance industry another curious and, perhaps, unique, method of distribution. It is called transshipping. A transshipper is a person or company that makes available to retailers just about any make or model of appliance or television set in single units or bulk lots.

Doing business with a transshipper rather than a distributor or manufacturer can be attractive to an appliance retailer for a number of reasons. He has access to lines for which he is not franchised, does not have to adhere to the quantity or mix requirements of a regular distributor, and he generally pays less money.

The disadvantages are absence of advertising funds, uncertain availability of parts and service, and lack of extended financing terms since all purchases are usually only for cash.

Transshippers get merchandise from distributors who are overstocked due to the quantities that the factories oblige them to take. Some transshippers operate a retail business only as a blind for buying through regular channels what they can't get *sub rosa*. They are able to undersell regular distribution channels for several reasons. They are permitted to net out or convert to cash the advertising money that normally accrues to each piece of merchandise and can make advantageous purchases when the market is glutted and a distributor needs cash quickly. Also, since they turn their stock rapidly and for cash, they are willing to work on very small profit margins. Quite often a transshipper will carry no inventory of his own, but will act as a broker between an anonymous distributor and the retailer.

Transshippers do business with everyone from stores whose small requirements would not enable them to be regularly franchised to the largest nationwide chains of mass merchandisers. The latter use transshippers to overcome the necessity of dealing with separate distributors in each of the markets where they have stores or because they are quite often able to pick up very attractive closeouts or "dumps."

The manufacturers and distributors are very much aware of the activities of the transshippers but are not inclined to do much about them. When business is slow they are a means of disposing of excess inventories. When business is good and merchandise is scarce, the transshippers are frozen out by their sources so that it is really not in a manufacturer's best interest to do away with them entirely. Their function is very much like that of snails in a fish tank.

From the standpoint of the customer, the refrigerator or television set he is contemplating purchasing has come a long, expensive way from the factory. Where economies in the process have been made or efficiencies achieved, very few of the dollars filter down to the buyer. The retailer, if he is sharp, enjoys some; the distributor and especially the factory get the most.

8

What's My Price?

ASIDE FROM THE choice of brand and model of a new appliance or television set, the consumer's most important consideration is the price he is going to pay for it. What he will pay is determined by how exhaustively he is willing to shop for an item, how aggressive he is as a trader, and, to a large extent, the brand of the article itself.

Unless he is affluent, it would be prudent to have a budget before committing himself to the purchase of a new appliance. If three hundred dollars is the limit, he would be wise to stick fairly rigidly within that limit. The seductive added-cost options such as automatic ice-makers, bleach dispensers, and remote control tend to make the investment go higher without significantly improving the basic usefulness or performance of an appliance.

Once the customer decides on a particular appliance, the customer will shop the available dealers in his market to learn if there is a spread among their prices. In an attempt to learn what is really the lowest price, the shopper will feel as though he has entered an Oriental bazaar. Prices will vary according to the markup philosophy of the store, how much the dealer's inventory is loaded, when the salesman made his last sale, even the way the customer is dressed. It is axiomatic among appliance salesmen that the sharpest customer and the one toughest to close is the "pipe smoker." This is the guy who reads *Consumer Reports*, has a Ph.D. in biochemistry, and wears tweed jackets with leather patches on the sleeves. He is especially frightening to sales people when he scribbles a verbatim account of the sales pitch in his tiny notebook. He can be counted upon to be quoted a lower price than the slob who walks in with his lunchbox under his arm.

The manufacturers have gone into markets where price cutting and sharp trading were endemic and turned the most flagrant discounters into choir boys. This was done by making a line go "fair trade." The fair-trade laws in many states permit a manufacturer to fix the minimum price at which his product can be sold at retail. These laws are binding upon a retailer whether or not he signs an agreement. As long as one retailer in his state has signed to maintain the fair-trade price, all others have to comply. In the states where these nonsigner fair-trade agreements are in effect, they are operative and have teeth.

From the customer's standpoint, fair trade forces him to pay a higher price than he might otherwise pay in a free market. For the retailer, it is supposed to protect his profit, but it restrains him from setting his own selling price on goods to which he has legal title. In a market like New York City it is almost impossible to buy any well-known make of appliance, television, or stereo set for less than the factory-established fair-trade price. This applies to Magnavox, Sylvania, Motorola, Frigidaire, Fedders, Westinghouse, General Electric, Hotpoint, Admiral, and many other lines. While RCA and Zenith are not fair-traded in New York City, the distributors of these lines choose to fair-trade them locally in the upstate New York counties they cover.

Consumers living near state borders can sometimes enjoy the best of two possible worlds. Zenith is fair-traded in New Jersey, but anyone can go to New York and make his own deal. It would seem that there is a basic unfairness in a law that permits a manufacturer to hold a club over the head of a retailer in one state while his competitor across the border can use the same weapon to beat his ears off. Conversely, the buyer residing in a state or county where prices are controlled by fair-trade laws is forced to pay more for the same equipment than in one where a manufacturer or distributor has not fair-traded his product.

Paul Dixon, former Chairman of the Federal Trade Commission and a self-avowed champion of the consumer, has called the fair-trade laws "the sorriest damn thing that ever came in America. The worst dealer gets a free ride on the good guy." He means, of course, that the law regulates the price that both the efficient, low-overhead dealer and the slipshod, high-overhead dealer must charge.

It is not entirely impossible to enjoy discounts on fair-traded merchandise. Price cutting does go on, and the manufacturers can police only a small segment of the dealer structure. Trade papers that circulate among appliance dealers continually cite cases where a manufacturer has gone to court to enjoin a retailer from cutting the price on his goods. These lawsuits are usually generated by a dealer complaining to a manufacturer that a competitor is cutting prices. The factory, if it is aggressively fair-trade-oriented, will send an operative of a shopping service or a private investigator to check out the complaint. He will endeavor to get a bill of sale on a fair-traded item showing a discounted price. He does this by telling a salesman anxious to make a sale that he can buy it for less down the street or by dangling a lump sum of cash that is just below the minimum fair-trade price.

Armed with the bill of sale, the manufacturer can go to court and get an injunction. First offenses are let off with a warning from the court if the dealer agrees not to continue to cut the price. Further violations, if proven, bring fines, as the dealer is then in contempt of court.

Some very large appliance retailers have been prosecuted, but rarely has one been cut off from a supplier for violating fair-trade pricing. Factories need strong outlets for their products more than they need legal victories.

If you are a regular customer and are known by the dealer or he is convinced that you are not a professional shopper, a small amount of price resistance on your part can sometimes secure discounts on fair-trade merchandise. This is particularly true in the case of limited franchise lines of television and stereo where profit margins are much more generous than they are on appliances.

Once you have determined the product you are going to buy and how much it will cost, the next question is, "How will I pay for it?" The two obvious choices are cash and some form of deferred payment. Many buyers have a natural and justifiable reluctance to pay cash for any appliance or television set, even if they have the money readily available. They have found, or fear, that once a dealer has the money in his cash register the customer will have a hard time obtaining service or adjustment if the new equipment proves faulty. Either they have been burned before or they have heard of others who have had this problem. The only way to be sure that complaints will be taken care of after the merchandise is paid for is to have unlimited confidence in the reputation and integrity of the dealer. Also, the customer is reasonably sure of not being left high and dry with a defective product if the service is being handled by an efficient, well-managed, factory-owned service branch.

The fact is, however, that a customer has much more leverage in dealing with initial failures, malfunctions, or defects in the finish such as scratches, blisters, or dents, if there is a substantial balance owed to the dealer. Once an appliance, television set, or stereo has been paid for or a conditional sales contract has been signed, the buyer's bargaining position is substantially weakened.

The ideal way of paying for an appliance from the customer's standpoint is to make a ninety-day deal. With this arrangement the buyer is expected to make a down payment of about 25 percent of the purchase price. Then he has ninety days in which to pay the balance in one lump sum or in three equal payments at thirty, sixty, and ninety days. This, of course, should be arranged so that there are no carrying charges added to the net cash price. If ninety-day terms are unavailable, the cash buyer should then try to secure a straight thirty-day charge. Generally, this type of purchase requires little or no cash down payment, and the merchandise is expected to be paid for in full thirty days after it is delivered.

Naturally, the dealer who accepts thirty- and ninety-day payment arrangements assumes that the buyer has a good credit rating. Dealers who do not make this type of deal will plead that the low prices they are charging preclude the expense of carrying their own accounts. They will offer as an alternative a short-term financing plan whereby the customer signs a conditional sales contract and repays a finance company in thirty, sixty, or ninety days, while the dealer receives his payment from the lending agency almost immediately. All finance companies make a charge for this service, and most dealers will attempt to pass it on to the buyer. If the dealer is hungry for the sale or if it is profitable enough he may be persuaded to absorb the charges himself.

Some large companies, like Sears, Montgomery Ward, and most department stores, offer a revolving credit plan. Here the buyer may pay in thirty days with no penalty or reduce his balance each month by an agreed amount, generally 10 percent, and pay a carrying charge on the outstanding balance. This charge is usually 1½ percent per month or an annual rate of 18 percent. Banks have recently become very active in this area of finance and have papered the country with their charge cards. Ecstatic over the relatively huge rates of interest this type of credit affords, the banks encourage the consumer to charge everything from gasoline to clothing, appliances, and even vacations on their credit cards. Not only is the return they receive from the retail customer extremely lucrative, but the banks also charge the store that takes a bank charge sale a fee ranging from 1 percent to 5 percent of the retail price, depending upon the volume of business the store furnishes the bank.

If the customer's budget or credit standing precludes paying off his purchase in a relatively short period of time, he must arrange to finance the deal on a long-term note. For most credit buyers this means signing a conditional sales contract, a type of promissory note in which the lender retains title to the merchandise until it is paid for. The dealer may sell this note to a bank or finance company and be paid for the merchandise almost immediately.

The store tries to assign these notes to the lender "without recourse," which means that the store does not guarantee payment to the bank or finance company in case the customer defaults. Now the seller is off the hook. He does not have to worry about collecting for the merchandise if the payments falter. It is the finance company's problem to dun, collect, or, if necessary, repossess the merchandise from delinquent accounts.

In addition, stores selling time-payment contracts to banks or finance companies generally receive a rebate or "kickback" of part of the interest charges. The amount of "kickback" the store enjoys on these time payment contracts varies from as little as 1 percent a year on the amount financed to as much as one-third of the total interest charged. Some appliance businesses derive a very substantial portion of their net profits from this "finance income."

Another pitfall involved in financing consumer durable goods is the effort of finance companies to sell insurance. For an added fee they will insure the payment of the outstanding balance in case of the death or incapacity of the borrower. Or they will cancel the balance due if the merchandise financed is lost, severely damaged, or destroyed by fire, flood, windstorm, etc. While the amounts charged for this insurance may seem small, they add up. The stores, of course, receive an extra commission for selling contracts with insurance.

Naturally, where such a risk-free profit opportunity presents itself, the stores endeavor to finance as many sales as possible and for the longest period of time. Some stores even pay a salesman a bonus if the contracts are written for more than twenty-four months. The dealers who can afford it do not sell all of these time-payment contracts to finance companies. They retain the good credit risks or the "cream" and collect these themselves, thereby enjoying the full proceeds of the finance charge. Many appliance and furniture establishments have set up in-house financing corporations to handle this profitable by-product of their retail business. Some stores are able to derive a greater net profit from financing than from the sale of the merchandise they are ostensibly in business to sell.

This type of financing carries extremely high rates of interest. Under the new truth-in-lending law, it is now apparent to the buyer that the true annual interest rate on many purchases exceeds 25 percent a year. The lending institutions attempt to justify these rates by citing the fact that the customers who buy this way are the marginal or poor credit risks. They are also the groups with limited income who can least afford to pay this heavy burden. Stores in ghetto areas dealing to a large degree with a Negro or Puerto Rican population have often gloated over the fact that they have been able to "lump up" their customers with high finance charges. They have taken advantage of the minority groups' lack of education, experience, and buying sophistication, and their limited access to credit, to unload goods at the highest prices and interest rates. Some furniture and appliance dealers, when discussing the way they have capitalized on this situation, refer to their black customers as "mah folks." Their attitude is a good reason why this kind of store has been a prime target for looting and burning during periods of civil disorder. Educational campaigns by government and interested private organizations are endeavoring to make the minority groups aware of the practices for which they have long been the "pigeons."

As much good as new legislation and public education has done, a great deal remains to be accomplished in the area of consumer awareness. State and federal truth-in-lending laws require that the seller fill in a sales contract in full before it is presented to the buyer for his signature. All information must be clearly filled in relating to an accurate description of the merchandise— the full purchase price, cash down payment, trade-in allowance, amount of interest charged, and true annual rate of interest. Unfortunately, many buyers still sign blank or incomplete contracts in their anxiety to get the merchandise. They are frequently under the impression that the seller is doing them a favor by extending credit.

Carrying charges can bring the total cost of a $300 refrigerator to more than $372 over the span of a two-year contract. Or, a $500 color television set comes to over $680 if financed for three years. It can therefore be seen that the consumer can save much more money by a careful consideration of payment plans than by fighting to get the last dollar's discount off the purchase price.

If a buyer cannot afford the full amount at the time of purchase, there are some less costly methods of securing credit terms. Many companies, government agencies, and religious or fraternal organizations operate credit unions. It is always less expensive to borrow from these federally or state-chartered groups than from commercial sources. Banks are usually just as willing to extend money on an unsecured personal note to creditworthy persons as they are to take the same note from a dealer. The advantages to the buyer are a lower rate of interest and title to the merchandise. This means that he is free to dispose of the item or move it to another state without first securing the approval of the lender on a conditional sales contract before it is fully paid for.

The financing end of the major appliance business has also proved alluring to most of the major appliance manufacturers. They are not content to leave this profitable area entirely to banks, local finance companies, or national outfits like Commercial Credit Corporation, Household Finance Corporation, or Universal CIT Credit Corporation.

Subsidiary consumer finance companies—GECC (General Electric Credit Corporation), WCC (Westinghouse Credit Corporation), GMAC (General Motors Acceptance Corporation)—are obvious examples of merchandising and financing tie-ins. The Whirlpool Corporation controls ABCC (Appliance Buyers Credit Corporation) and Kelvinator (American Motors) owned Redisco. Norge operated through BWAC (Borg-Warner Acceptance Corporation).

Factories may claim that they operate their finance-company subsidiaries in order to facilitate the wholesale and retail sales of their products. However, in no case where they are extending credit to the consumer do they offer any lower interest rates than can be obtained from other lenders. They usually operate at or near the maximum rate in each state.

Aside from the lucrative business of financing consumer purchases of appliances, furniture, and other home furnishings, these captive companies serve their parent companies in another important area: the financing of dealers' purchases from the factory or distributor.

In almost no other business is it possible for a retailer

to get so much merchandise with so little equity in it. These credit arms of the factory make it possible for a dealer to buy on "floor plan" large amounts of goods with little or no cash investment. Floor planning involves selling a dealer merchandise without giving him title to it. Since the goods are really only "loaned" to the dealer, he is obliged to pay for them as soon as they are sold.

The sales force of the appliance companies use this easy access to credit to promote the sale of their lines. Retailers are regularly offered ninety days of interest-free floor planning; when new lines are shown or when goods back up and have to be moved, interest-free terms up to six months are common.

If a dealer is actively selling the goods bought on this arrangement and is liquid enough to pay for them as they are sold, the plan is a real merchandising aid. If, however, the merchandise remains unsold at the expiration date of the interest-free period, the retailer must either pay for it in full or renew his note on it and pay finance charges that may exceed his net profit when he finally does sell it.

If a dealer's inventory becomes loaded with floor-planned merchandise as a result of overbuying or sales poorer than anticipated, he really has a serious problem. He is faced with the prospect of having to come up with the cash to pay for it in full at the expiration date of the three-month free ride or, if he can, reduce the indebtedness by 10 or 20 percent and pay a stiff interest charge on the balance.

Under these circumstances, many dealers will grab almost any deal in order to unload slow-moving merchandise and raise cash in a hurry. The customer who happens to fall onto a hard-pressed merchant will sometimes be offered truly spectacular buys even on fair-traded merchandise.

Such situations are rarely recognized by the consumer, as there are many more factors operating to raise the price he pays than there are to reduce it. Remembering to shop objectively and unemotionally, remaining within a realistic budget, avoiding the switch to an unasked-for brand, and scrutinizing finance charges will provide more consistent value for the consumer's dollar than the rare real bargain.

9

From This
They Make a Living?

THE RETAIL DEALER derives a relatively small markup on the sale of a nationally branded major appliance. The profit margins range from as little as 20 percent or less on the lower-priced "leader" models to a maximum of about 30 percent on the high-priced "deluxe" models. This contrasts with retail markups of 35 to 50 percent and more on furniture.

Why does a man go into a business that ostensibly shows so little profit potential? There are several reasons. First, as we have pointed out earlier, it has not been a difficult business to get into. The factories, through their captive financing companies, make it easy to stock a store through the use of "floor plan" arrangements. That is, with little or no cash investment a dealer has the merchandise in his store and doesn't have to pay for it for three to six months or until it is sold.

Second, dealers are persuaded by the factory and distributor salesmen that percentage markup doesn't mean anything. The manufacturers seduce the dealers by emphasizing gross dollar profits per sale of $50, $75, or $100. They tell the dealers the thing to bear in mind is gross dollars. "You go to the bank with dollars, not percentage points," has been their enlistment slogan for years.

This argument was promulgated by Walter C. Fisher, President of Zenith Sales Corporation in an interview reported in the July 28, 1969, issue of *Home Furnishings Daily*. In an oblique effort to defend Zenith's historically low retail margins, Fisher said, "You can make some very fine buys that look like an excellent gross [profit].

"Nothing happens, however, until the merchandise turns [sells] and you convert the percentage into cash. I've never yet found a man who can take a percentage of profit to the bank."

The fact Mr. Fisher chooses to ignore is that although Zenith has increased its share of the color television business to the point where it is hot on the heels of RCA, the greatest strides in the past few years have been made by the lines that have improved their profitability to the dealer. Shrewd appliance dealers stock and advertise both Zenith and RCA to develop traffic to their stores, where they take the opportunity to try to switch the customers to more profitable lines like Magnavox and Sylvania.

A dealer might be able to make a living by keeping his overhead low, having his wife work in the business, and buying new merchandise only when a piece is sold. However, the squeeze between low retail margins and constantly rising costs has forced many appliance dealers to seek other merchandise offering greater profit potential. That is why a large number of appliance dealers have begun to sell furniture. Others offer complete kitchen-planning services, making a package of the appliances, cabinets, and sink and the accompanying electrical, plumbing, and carpentry work.

Who are the appliance dealers who make money, take on new lines, enlarge their stores, or open new stores? They are the dealers who have been able to control their expenses in the initial years of their business growth and have learned how to maximize the profit potential of each sale.

The successful dealers seek to sell the appliance lines that offer above-average markup and reward the salesmen who can sell them. They aggressively "sell up" to the higher-priced models, where the real profit lies. And they are able to make plus dollars by charging a customer for the "extras" that other dealers give away.

The appliance manufacturers recognize that it is almost impossible for a dealer to make a reasonable net profit or to grow on the profit margins they have built into their wholesale pricing. A recent dealer meeting of a factory-owned distributorship in the South was devoted to educating its dealers on how to "trade up" to the more profitable models and how to increase their net profit margins by 25 percent or more.

The first pitchman explained how to promote a fifteen-cubic-foot refrigerator with an ice maker that everyone would be happy to sell at $349 and make a $100 gross profit. He pointed out that advertising this box in the newspaper at $349, as good as it was, would not bring too many customers into a dealer's store. But, he said, if the dealers advertised another refrigerator that appeared similar, also with an ice maker, for $288.88, the customers would think it was a real deal and come flying in for it.

What the customer looking to buy this refrigerator for $288.88 would not know was that in small print in the ad the dealer showed a model number. This model number would tell the initiated that the "bargain" model was a last year's fourteen-cubic-foot model in avocado green with a left-hand door. As if that were not unattractive enough, the dealer was instructed to show it on his floor with the wooden shipping skids still on the bottom and the cardboard packing and tape left in the interior.

Next, the dealer was told to show on his floor a slightly better looking fourteen-cubic-foot model for $318. He was told to tell his customers that for only $30 more than the unappealing advertised model they could have a choice of color and door swing and a slightly more dressed up refrigerator.

This pitch was all a prelude or "stepup" to the real "sell model," the $349 job, that the dealer wanted to sell in the first place. It was recommended by the factory-employed sales trainer that the dealer show this refrigerator in a well-lit area with a spotlight on it if possible. The model should be plugged in so that the interior light would go on when the door was opened. The automatic ice maker was to be hooked up and working, and the interior loaded with dummy food. In this theatrical setting and after looking at the plain, stripped-down models, $349 should look like a bargain and the sale should be made.

At this point, the store salesman is told to attempt to mollify the reluctant customer, who is now $60 over the price she came prepared to pay. "After all," he murmurs philosophically, "you only buy a refrigerator once every fifteen or twenty years. Why not get one you really like? The payments will only be $2 a month more." For thirty-six months, that is!

After this eye-opener, the branch sales manager got up and said that he was going to educate the group of dealers present on how to raise their net profit by 25 percent. He explained net profit this way: "It's what you have left down on the bottom line, after you've paid your expenses, taken out a living for yourself, and paid your taxes. It's the money you use to expand your business, open another store, or send your kids to college."

He then asked rhetorically, "How many of you dealers are charging extra for color in refrigeration?" When no one raised his hand, he yelled, "You're throwing away money!" To dramatize his point he began to fling crumpled-up dollar bills at the audience.

"How many of you try to sell wheels with refrigerators? How many collect for hooking up an ice maker? Are you trying to sell second-year service policies?" Negative responses to these queries brought a further shower of crumpled greenbacks—all money that the dealers were obviously letting slip through their grasp.

To illustrate his thesis that net profit could be raised substantially, the speaker referred to a chart on which the profit structure of the previously mentioned $349 refrigerator was broken down. As can be seen from chart A (opposite), by selling the extras a dealer could net twice as much money as on selling the refrigerator alone!

CHART A. REFRIGERATOR MODEL XYZ

	COST	RETAIL	GROSS PROFIT
	$249	$349	$100

Average *net* profit of appliance dealers, 6% (high)—$21

	COST	SELL	NET PROFIT
Color	$3	$ 7	$ 4
Wheels	$6	$12	$ 6
Ice Maker Hook-up (Labor and Tubing)	$6	$21	$15
2nd-Year Warranty		$17	$17
	$15	$57	$42

Chart B shows the additional profit opportunity in selling an electric dryer. The net profit to the dealer is $42.25, or more than five times what he realizes from the sale of the dryer alone!

CHART B. DRYER MODEL ABC

	COST	RETAIL	NET PROFIT
	$105	$139	$34
Net profit on sale @ 6%—$8.40			
Dryer Cord	$ 1.50	$ 5.00	$ 3.50
Dryer Rack	$ 4.25	$ 8.00	$ 3.75
2nd-Year Warranty	$ 0.00	$15.00	$15.00
Vent Kit	$ 2.50	$ 7.50	$ 5.00
Labor (Venting)	$ 2.50	$ 7.50	$ 5.00
Wiring	$30.00	$40.00	$10.00
	$40.75	$83.00	$42.25

Examples of other opportunities for capturing more profit on the sale of an appliance were:

1. Charge extra for special orders.

2. Charge for delivery and setting up of special sale or clearance items.

3. Sell factory-labeled detergent for $5.95 at a cost of $3.00.

4. Sell fabric-softener dispensers at $5.95 at a cost of $3.00.

5. Sell Teflon griddles for stoves.

6. Sell aluminum foil for oven liners.

7. Sell additional ice cube trays with refrigerators.

8. Sell porcelain meat pans for refrigerators not equipped with them.

The attending dealers, now awed by the prospect of huge new sources of profit, were then told that they had nothing to worry about in charging for all these things. "Your competition is getting it. Sears, Roebuck sells its second-year service policy like a religion and is successful in selling it in over 70 percent of appliance sales. They've even gone to selling third- and fourth-year warranties!"

A former Sears salesman in the audience conveniently verified the fact that Sears was more apt to dismiss a salesman who sold $300,000 worth of appliances with no second-year warranties than one who sold only $170,-000 worth but was able to sell the warranty 90 percent of the time.

The observation was made at this meeting that perhaps it was less than ethical for a factory to encourage sharp practices as a means of dealer survival in the face of the low gross profits that factory pricing dictated. The speaker replied, "Hell, when a friend asks that lady who bought the dryer with $90 worth of extras what she paid for it, she'll say, '$139'!"

The manufacturers are aware of the extreme pressure that the small profit margin inherent in the appliance business exerts upon the dealers. Figures released by Jules Steinberg, executive secretary of NARDA (National Appliance and Radio/Television Dealers' Association), reveal that in 1968 the average net profit reported by the association's members was less than 1 percent. The 6 percent net profit figure thrown out by the factory representative in this sales meeting is wildly unrealistic.

The companies in strong marketing positions—Frigidaire, General Electric, Maytag, RCA, Zenith—simply urge their dealers to sell more units. They claim that the additional volume generated will make up for thin profit margins. Other firms—Admiral, Philco, Gibson, Olympic,

Norge—try to structure their wholesale prices with more generous margins. A dealer selling their products at somewhere near the factory's suggested retail price will generally come out with a higher markup.

Most dealers feel that they are entitled to a better profit when selling a secondary line because they have to work harder for it. Either they had to spend more money advertising that line to get people into their stores, or they had to spiff their salesmen liberally to induce them to switch the customers into the more profitable goods.

The retail customer is seldom aware of his own power to avoid getting loaded with extra charges when he buys a major appliance. The business is so brutally competitive that anyone who takes a firm stand against being charged for service he expected to get for nothing will usually prevail. In an effort to move the merchandise, a store will take a close deal and hope it will be able to make it up by lumping the next customer.

The promotion of second-year service policies is the area that represents the greatest opportunity for profit beyond the sale of the appliance itself. Sears, Roebuck has been most successful in exploiting this field. Since Sears maintains a costly service setup doing mostly no-charge in-warranty work, anything that will contribute income to the service operation is welcome. Sears salesmen are constantly drilled to push second-year service policies. They point out that although the service is free for the first year, all sorts of chilling and pocketbook-paralyzing things can happen after the free service period expires. "Suppose the washer transmission conks out or the refrigerator compressor goes into cardiac arrest? You could be looking at an $80 repair bill. Why not insure yourself against this just as you insure your house or car—or even your life?"

Sears' salesmen have even subtly suggested that a request for service by a second-year contract holder will get dispatched quicker than one from the cheap guy who didn't see fit to buy the contract.

Everyone knows that the only kind of insurance that someone is surely going to collect on is life insurance. If the odds against the type of expensive failures alluded to by the people at Sears and elsewhere were endemic, it would be actuarily unsound to promote the policies. It is only the insecure person who has no confidence in his buying decision that lets himself be frightened or bullied into purchasing extended insurance coverage.

A few television dealers will try to sell some kind of extra-cost service protection for the first ninety days after a television set is delivered. While some television manufacturers are experimenting with burying this charge in the selling price, the prevalent industry custom is to make the initial setup and ninety-day service the responsibility of the dealer.

If a dealer is maintaining his own service shop, he will try to sell a service contract for the balance of the first year after the initial ninety-day period. He will do this to secure additional revenue to offset his service costs, and to avoid performing the service for nothing, which is what he would have had to do anyway if a customer screamed loud enough or refused to pay.

The most lucrative item for extra income in the sale of a television set—especially a color set—is the sale of an elaborate antenna system. While it is true that a good antenna will enhance color television reception, any antenna that is providing a satisfactory, snow-free signal on black and white is perfectly suitable for color. Yet customers are told that they should have a new antenna if they want to enjoy their color set. These antenna systems are sold for upwards of $150 if a directional rotor is called for. This installation should not cost a dealer much more than $90 if he farms the work out to an antenna specialist, and much less if he or his own staff does the work. The best antenna hardware comprising everything needed for a $150 UHF-VHF antenna on a rotor should be able to be bought for between $60 and $75. This is an area where a "do-it-yourselfer" who is not squeamish about walking around on his roof can save a lot of money.

The customer should bear in mind that if he is not doing business with the only store in town he should stand his ground. He can get his ice maker connected, his dryer vented, or the "pigtail" cord for his electric range installed either at no charge or for a lot less than was originally asked for these trimmings. All it takes is the true shopper's stamina and the poker player's bluff.

10

Private Label, or
"I Got It at Sears"

To MOST PEOPLE who are not in the trade, the news that Sears, Roebuck sells almost as many refrigerators as Frigidaire or General Electric and more washers and dryers than Maytag and Whirlpool combined would come as quite a surprise. In spite of the coast-to-coast distribution and the extensive advertising campaigns devoted to these branded lines, Sears consistently outsells them in market after market. Since more people are buying the Sears Kenmore washers and dryers and Coldspot refrigerators are capturing a very large percentage of the market, it will be useful to find out why.

First of all, Sears is 100 percent dedicated to the marketing of huge quantities of major appliances. It has developed a vertically integrated marketing system that encompasses the manufacture, distribution, sales, financing, and servicing of nearly everything sold in the major-appliance category. This includes sales in the major-appliance departments of Sears' full-line department stores and catalogue stores, and mail order.

Sears has only recently reduced its major stock holdings in the Whirlpool Corporation, which produces most of its refrigeration products and all of its home laundry equipment. Sears holds 48 percent of the stock of the Roper Company. Roper manufactures all of Sears' gas and electric ranges and holds contracts to produce rotary lawn mowers, drapery hardware, and venetian blinds for Sears. Whirlpool and Roper claim that Sears does not enjoy any spectacular buying advantage. However, with 58 percent of Whirlpool's total output and 75 percent of Roper's range business going to Sears, it would be easy to believe otherwise. Many thoughtful appliance dealers begrudge Whirlpool and Roper the business they give them because they feel that the higher prices they pay are subsidizing the lower prices charged to Sears.

Although these semicaptive companies can justify charging Sears less because of huge commitments for future production, these efficiencies never seem to be reflected in the prices charged to other accounts. The wholesale prices of Whirlpool and Roper products distributed through regular channels are never any less than competitive lines of any other nationally branded appliances.

By dominating the production of these factories Sears is able to have first call on technical or design innovations and reserves for its models the most desirable features. Kenmore washers had self-cleaning lint filters before they were available on Whirlpool machines. All Kenmore dryers have had drop-down-loading doors for years, but it is only recently that Whirlpool has made them available —on its more expensive models. Adjustable refrigerator shelves were a feature of some Coldspot refrigerators for some time before they made their appearance in a Whirlpool refrigerator. This is an area other than price in which Sears has used its great power to the disadvantage of dealers selling the nationally branded lines of these factories.

144

Most of Sears' television sets not subcontracted to Japanese manufacturers are made by the Warwick Electronics Company in Chicago. Warwick is a publicly owned corporation, and a large portion of its stock is held by the Whirlpool Corporation and Sears. For the last several years Warwick has reported annual losses of between $3 and $4 million. The smaller stockholders in Warwick might be persuaded that Sears was willing to take losses in Warwick to underwrite unrealistically low retail prices on Silvertone television sets. Since Silvertone has had to fight to get an important share of the color television market, this might well be Sears' method of making that penetration.

Regardless of the economies Sears can make in the purchasing of its major appliances, it is in the ability to move these goods at retail that the company really excels. Sears has refined the bait-and-switch technique of advertising to the point where its competition is almost helpless. It has advertised an automatic washer complete with matching electric dryer, at a price of $177 for both pieces. When a shopper recently rushed into his nearest Sears store to snap up this obvious bargain, this is what happened:

The shopper was approached immediately by a salesman, and the advertised "special" was shown to him. The washer and dryer were prominently displayed with a sign indicating that $177 was the sale price for both units. When the customer asked how soon the items could be delivered, the salesman replied that the dryer was available right away but the washers were "sold out." The customer asked how long it would be before the washers would be back in stock and the salesman said that he didn't know, "it was up to the warehouse."

After the shopper confessed that it was really the washer he needed, as his old machine had just broken down, the salesman really went to work. He explained that the advertised model, although it washed clothes, lacked water-temperature regulation, had to be watched during the fill cycle if less than a full tub was needed, and didn't have any provision for the special washing action that synthetic fabrics, delicate things, or permanent-press garments needed. Also, the top of the machine was painted enamel rather than porcelain and in time would rust or discolor.

All of these drawbacks were not hard to believe since the machine looked, at best, rudimentary. "But," the salesman continued, as he glided over to a flashy machine in the next row, "here's a three-speed, ten-cycle, all-push-button model that we have on special for only $259." When told by the customer that $259 was a lot more than he expected to pay, the salesman took the shopper into his confidence.

"Look," he said, "here's another machine that's also on sale this week. It's regularly $229.95, but we have a few left that the store is letting go for only $198. It's a two-speed, five-cycle model with the good lint filter and, confidentially, it will do everything the $259 machine will do except that you'll have to turn a few knobs instead of pushing a couple of buttons."

Close examination of the $198 washer proved it to be a sound and useful machine and a good, if not spectacular, value. Of course, it was still $21 more than the washer and dryer on the combination deal that brought the customer into the store. What Sears had done was to bring people into the store with the bait, make the bait model unattractive and unavailable, show a high-priced deluxe model, and then switch to the sell model.

The rest of the appliance industry's frustration with these tactics was evidenced a few years ago when Westinghouse produced a training film for retail salesmen. The film, shown at sales training sessions and even carried to dealers' stores, depicted a situation in a Sears store very much like the foregoing example of the Sears advertising and sales pitch. Its purpose was to make salesmen competing with Sears aware of the methods used, and to educate them to do the same. Tied in with the film was a merchandising program for which Westinghouse made available a stripped-down washer which dealers were to advertise at a price not much more than their cost. It was hoped that by using this "dog" for bait, Westinghouse dealers would have the opportunity to practice the same sales methods that Sears was using so successfully against them.

In the long run these efforts to fight Sears on its own level rarely do the job. Independent retailers and other chains cannot seem to commit themselves to a sustained high-pressure sales effort. As distinct from the Sears salesmen, other retailers' allegiance is divided among several makes, and their sales training, promotion, and goals are fragmented. At Sears, the appliance sales people undergo an intensive and continuous sales training program. Since Sears has only one line to sell, the salesmen are expected to know everything about it down to the last nut and bolt. Practically every Sears store has a classroom where these training sessions are held and the individual salesman's progress is recorded. He is expected to know not only the strong points of his own product inside out but also the weaknesses of competing brands. A retail customer can generally learn a lot more about what he is buying from a salesman at Sears than from someone on just about any other sales floor in America.

Until recently Sears has been able to attract above-average sales people and, more important, keep the turnover of salesmen to a minimum. This was accomplished by paying a liberal commission and tying them into the Sears profit-sharing program. Under this plan a Sears employee accrues dividends in the form of stock, plus contributions by the company to a generous retirement plan. After five or six years' involvement in this program many employees feel that they simply cannot afford to leave Sears in view of the long-term benefits they would have to forfeit.

NARDA, the independent appliance dealers' association, has blown the whistle several times on the alleged misleading character of Sears' advertising. In complaints to the Federal Trade Commission, NARDA has cited as examples the automatic-washer ads (one ad in an Illinois newspaper offered a big "frostless" refrigerator for $199 which proved in the store to be not frost-free). Jules Steinberg, NARDA spokesman, is quoted in *Home Furnishings Daily* to the effect that surveys have shown that 60 percent of major appliance customers buy in the first store they visit. "All we want is an equal chance to sell the customer," he declared.

In the financing of appliance sales Sears also has an advantage over independents. It offers a thirty-day charge plan at no interest, which is an accommodation that would seriously strap some less well capitalized businesses. If a purchase is going to be financed, Sears has the additional opportunity to make a lucrative profit by putting the sale through its own finance company. The charges for this service are 1½ percent per month on the unpaid balance —or a true annual interest rate of 18 percent. While many consumer finance companies charge higher rates, money is still available at banks and credit unions for less. A citizen in Sioux Falls, South Dakota, brought suit in July 1969 against Sears, Montgomery Ward, and J. C. Penney Company charging that the 18 percent annual rate is usurious since South Dakota's laws prohibit anyone from charging more than 8 percent. If his suit is successful it may open the door to customers to recover the finance charges collected by those companies.

Another reason for Sears' success in the appliance business is that it has, in the last ten years or so, built its big stores where the people are, and with its smaller units and catalogue outlets even where the customers aren't. In the Greater Los Angeles market, Sears' twenty-one department stores and twenty-eight satellite appliance stores are estimated to do 25 percent of the $200-million-a-year appliance business. While Sears' penetration in other markets might not be as great, it dominates just about every area in the retailing of major appliances.

Sears has taken aggressive steps to upgrade a previously poor service image. First it set up large service facilities in metropolitan centers to cover a fairly wide geographical area. Next, it gradually installed fully staffed service branches in outlying stores to bring the service people closer to their customers and shorten the waiting times these customers formerly experienced. It is interesting to note that when Sears is about to open a major store in a new market, it advertises to recruit service people just as aggressively as it does for sales people.

One of the few opportunities Sears leaves to smaller

dealers to compete with it is in the matter of delivery. Anyone seeking same-day delivery is out of luck. The sheer size of the operation and the need to schedule deliveries from local and regional warehouses at least several days in advance precludes individual service. Aside from its inability to make emergency deliveries, Sears quite often is unable to deliver appliances for lengthy periods, because of lack of stock. No one could expect Sears to plan the sales movement of individual items so as to have the right quantity, size, style, and color of every appliance in each warehouse, and a great deal of time can pass before these out-of-stock items or special orders can be shipped from factories or large-inventory depots.

Independent appliance dealers try to avoid a long hiatus between sale and delivery by first pushing the goods they own. If that fails, they can usually draw from a local distributor in a day or so or even pick up a piece from a competitor. This sort of swapping goes on all the time among dealers who are willing to pay another dealer a few dollars extra rather than blow a sale on an item they don't have or a line for which they may not be franchised. Then the smaller store will get the appliance on its own truck and out to the customer who had to have it the same day.

It is this aggressiveness or tenacity that enables independent appliance dealers to compete with Sears. Quite often they will discover through conversation with a customer browsing in their stores that the shopper has already bought an appliance from Sears and has been waiting several weeks for delivery. In a situation like this, a creative salesman will first sympathize with the customer and then arouse his indignation. If the salesman can raise the customer's boiling point high enough he can frequently switch the customer to what his store sells, with a promise of immediate delivery. Then he watches gleefully as the customer marches back to Sears for a refund of his deposit.

This approach would probably never sway a deepdyed, long-time Sears customer. That loyal group of shoppers devoted to Sears wouldn't even dream of looking elsewhere for an appliance. They have confidence in the image of bigness, they make a religion of buying only at Sears, and their revolving charge accounts go round and round.

Sears' next effort to corner even a larger share of the appliance business is in raising the status of its privatelabel brands. Even now, with the millions of Sears appliances in American homes, a Kenmore washer, a Coldspot refrigerator, or a Silvertone television set lacks a class image. For years these were the makes you bought when you couldn't afford a Maytag, Frigidaire, Zenith, or RCA. To combat this economy or utilitarian image, Sears first of all upgraded its styling. Kenmore washers now have fourteen push buttons against an industry high of ten, Coldspot refrigerators are shown with black vinyl exteriors trimmed with brass and displaying the designer's signature on a metal plate affixed to the box, like the legend tacked onto the frame of a museum painting.

Sears has taken a glamour feature like an automatic ice maker and pushed it for all it's worth. All but the lowest-price refrigerators in the Coldspot line now offer this gadget, which other lines still treat as an extra-cost luxury. Along with jazzed-up product design, the appearance of the Sears stores themselves has changed. The stodgy, cramped downtown stores with their emphasis on tires, motor oil, fertilizer, and fencing are being phased out. In their place have come huge, modern department stores in the best shopping center and mall locations. In these stores the accent on fashion in ready-to-wear and home furnishings carries over into the appliance departments and tends to create a livelier atmosphere.

As these Sears superstores continue to proliferate, the service and distribution operations improve, and the thrust of a more daring design concept is developed, Sears' position in the appliance business will become even more firmly entrenched.

Montgomery Ward is still a distant second behind Sears in the race between the giants in the private label sector of the industry. The Ward's Signature brand of appliances and Ward's Airline television sets, radios, and phonographs are, like the Sears appliances, all made by well-known brand-name manufacturers. Ward's refrigerators, freezers, and air conditioners are built by Frigidaire and Gibson and Ward's laundry equipment is made by the Norge division of the Fedders Corporation. Television sets not imported from Japan are now supplied by a subsidiary of Admiral Corp.

It should be noted that Sears' and Ward's appliance salesmen are not above pointing out product similarities and price differences between the private label brands they sell and the nationally-branded lines of the manufacturers who make them. They will ask a customer, quite justifiedly sometimes, "Why should you pay more for a Whirlpool washer or refrigerator when our Kenmore or Coldspot is the same product for less money?"

Westinghouse dealers chafed uncomfortably when

Ward's advertised refrigerators (produced by Westinghouse and quite similar to their regular models) for less than these dealers were paying wholesale. Complaints to Westinghouse or Whirlpool or any other manufacturer who produces for private label never receive a satisfactory reply. The manufacturers take refuge in legal double-talk, saying that they have no control over the prices that these private-label customers charge. This, of course, doesn't prevent the manufacturers from fair-trading, or fixing the retail prices of the dealers who compete with private label. When a manufacturer does this, he is in effect putting an umbrella over the private-label brand and sheltering it from competition. The brand-name retailers are forced to maintain price on merchandise very like private label in all major respects except the brand name stuck on it.

The Montgomery Ward approach to the appliance business has not been nearly as dynamic as Sears'. Until quite recently, along with a change of top management, but before its consolidation with the Container Corporation of America, Ward's began to cut back on small, older stores and follow Sears into putting up large full-line department stores in shopping-center locations. Ward's advertising was more forthright, as it traditionally did not promote only the leader models but exposed the customer to the trade-up goods with the "good-better-best" formula. If it wished to emulate Sears, perhaps it would have done better to leave the stepups to professionally trained and adequately motivated sales people.

While Montgomery Ward is making progress in becoming a more important factor in appliance marketing, it still has a lot of catching up to do. It will be some time before its sales, service, and distributive effort can overtake a Sears that seems to be running faster all the time.

Three other giant retail chains which have an impact on the sales of major appliances are J. C. Penney, W. T. Grant, and Western Auto Stores. Penney's Pencrest line of appliances are made by the Hotpoint division of General Electric, Grant's Bradford and Western's Wizard lines are made by companies like the Franklin Manufacturing Company, which specialize almost exclusively in producing for private label.

Compared with Sears and Montgomery Ward, the appliance business being done by Penney and Grant seems puny. However, along with Western Auto they will become a factor because of sheer weight of numbers. Each of these chains has well over a thousand stores from coast to coast and has well-financed and aggressive expansion plans. In the next few years they will become a significant factor in appliance distribution.

The large traditional department stores in the United States, especially those affiliated with the Federated, Allied, City Store, or Macy's buying groups, have all crept under the private-label tent. Department stores have been complaining for years that their appliance departments do not give them sufficient markup. Appliance-industry spokesmen, on the other hand, have chastised the department stores' hidebound attitude toward what they consider a reasonable percentage of profit. They accuse these stores of letting the appliance business slip away to the discount chains and the appliance specialty stores.

Rather than slugging it out pricewise with the discounters on branded lines, the department stores have

154

installed their own brands of appliances. Counting on either customers' loyalty or blind faith, they apparently believe that this is the only means they have to protect their sacred profit margins. Aside from private-label appliances, the department stores have all flocked to price-maintained television and stereo lines like Magnavox, Sylvania, and Motorola. They are satisfied to stay in the appliance business to serve their customers if they can do it at or near traditional department store markups. They are willing to forego the areas in which they would be forced to be competitive.

The major discount chains, such as K-Mart, Woolco, Zayre's, Two Guys, and Korvette's are still too young to succeed with private-label appliances. Their image was built by hacking away at the price structures of nationally branded lines. They have not been in business long enough to give stability or create a value image on a major appliance with their own name on it. Korvette tried private label with its Kor-Val brand of appliances, but had very indifferent success.

The whole area of private-label merchandise poses serious problems for the appliance industry and a dilemma for the customer. The manufacturers enjoy it because it gives them additional production economies and levels out their production scheduling, and they can sell a large portion of their output with no promotional or distribution expense. The merchants who are able to sell private-label appliances derive an above-average profit return; and if the product performs well, they have a captive customer seeking other items which are sold exclusively by the private-label chain.

Appliance dealers who merchandise brand-name lines in competition with strong private-label goods have a problem. Indiscriminate factory franchising gives them little to call their own. The store on the next corner is sharp-shooting his price and cutting into his profit on the same-model refrigerator or television set, while a similar model is sold with a private label, as at Sears, at a nice protected profit.

The consumer obviously has a much wider choice among the nationally advertised brand-name goods. The only good reasons for him to buy private-label appliances would be:

1. If he were convinced that the private-label item was equal in quality to branded appliances.

2. If after shopping out the branded lines he found that the private label cost substantially less.

3. If he had more confidence in the private-label retailer's ability to fulfill promptly and competently his delivery and service commitments.

11

Unsafe on Any Channel

On May 17, 1967, the General Electric Company sent out a press release to the major news services in the United States. This bulletin caused the greatest furor over product safety in the history of the home-appliance industry. The release stated that General Electric had become aware that up to ninety thousand of its 1967 "C" line eighteen- and twenty-three-inch color television receivers were capable of emitting harmful levels of X-radiation.

The repercussions were immediate, and they are still being felt. First, sales of color television sets fell off. Next, set owners besieged dealers and servicemen seeking assurance that the sets in their homes were safe. The press fanned the affair by citing the possible danger of sterility or mutation in the genes of the offspring of this generation's television viewers. Then, belatedly, the federal government stepped in.

With the usual affinity for a cause that will make headlines, the politicians demanded that Congress enact legislation to limit the amount of radiation a television set was allowed to emit. Out of this, the Bureau of Radiological Health within the Department of Health, Education, and Welfare was assigned the task of drawing up standards to which the radiation output of TV sets should conform.

In the meantime, General Electric took quick and positive action to correct this possibly dangerous condition. Literature was mailed to thousands of television dealers and servicemen with information on how to identify the sick sets and how to eliminate the hazard. Dealers were asked to submit the names and addresses of customers owning these sets, in the hope that adequate records had been kept. As the sets were located either in customers' homes or in dealer or distributor inventories, General Electric sent technicians to modify them. Since the serial numbers of all the suspect sets in this batch were known, General Electric kept a tally on the field reports as the sets were fixed, and checked them off against factory records. At this date all but a handful of these sets have been accounted for and the corrections made.

These General Electric color sets, like all television sets produced for sale in the United States, had been tested by the Underwriters Laboratories and carried that agency's UL label of approval. However, the sets which gave rise to the problem were the result of production changes in the middle of the model year; it was not thought necessary to have them retested by Underwriters Laboratories. Since the General Electric sets did carry the UL label, the Underwriters Laboratories made an effort to assist General Electric in locating the sets. Underwriters Laboratories sent letters to fire marshals in cities and towns all over the country. They asked the cooperation of the local fire marshals in finding and reporting the sets to UL and said that they in turn would pass the information on to General Electric. The hunt took on the aspect of a search for a typhoid carrier.

The reason this particular group of color television sets had the potential to produce a dangerous level of X-radiation was the failure of a new type of high-voltage-regulator tube to function properly. All large-screen color receivers are required to generate approximately 25,000 volts in order to provide sufficient brightness on the picture-tube face. The purpose of the high-voltage-regulator tube is to monitor this voltage and prevent it from exceeding design limits. If the tube fails to perform properly or the voltage settings are tampered with, voltages can creep up to 28,000 volts or higher. At these voltages X rays are generated that are more powerful than the shielding built into the television set can cope with.

Although the burden of adverse publicity was focused on General Electric in this affair, the other television manufacturers hastily re-examined their products. Each of them sent letters to dealers assuring them that their production was continuously monitored to detect and correct above-normal radiation levels before the sets left the factories. They also sent bulletins warning television servicemen to check carefully the high-voltage levels on all color sets whenever they had the opportunity. Also, they admonished them never to advance the high-voltage adjustments beyond the recommended settings. This was sometimes done to coax more brightness from the color picture tube.

Although the American public became aware in May 1967 that a possible radiation hazard existed, it took the United States Congress until October 1968 to pass its

Federal Radiation Standards law. The purpose of this law was to set minimum standards for equipment capable of emitting radiation. Manufacturers of this equipment would be required to conform to these standards, and any articles produced before the guidelines went into effect and found to be hazardous would have to be repaired or replaced at the manufacturer's expense.

Not much was done to implement this law until in April 1969, Representatives Benjamin Rosenthal and Edward Koch, both New York Democrats, called upon the Federal Trade Commission and the United States Surgeon General to take action. Their demands were spurred by the results of a survey of five thousand color television sets in homes in Suffolk County, New York. The survey showed that 20 percent of these sets were emitting X rays above the danger level.

The actions the two congressmen sought were:

1. Requiring color-set manufacturers to inspect all color sets in homes or call them back to the factory for inspection.

2. Installation of radiation detectors on all new color television sets.

3. Compelling manufacturers to furnish these detection devices at no charge for sets already in homes.

4. Use of newspaper, radio, and television media by the FTC, the U.S. Public Health Service, and the manufacturers to alert the public to the possible danger and advise the public whom to call to have their sets checked.

Although these demands were far-reaching, they seemed to cause shudders only within the industry. Nothing further happened until late in May 1969, when Representative Paul Rogers (D., Florida) a cosponsor of the 1968 law, asked why the law was not being enforced. The agency concerned, the Department of Health, Education, and Welfare, replied that it could not do anything until specific standards were set. In June 1969, HEW announced that a committee had been formed to set technical standards; its report, due in July, was finally released on August 15, 1969.

The committee, composed of representatives from government, industry, and the public (mostly scientists), established fixed goals for the manufacturers. By January 1970, television receivers must be built so that radiation would not exceed .5 milliroentgens per hour about two inches from any point accessible to a viewer. This requirement was to be reduced to .1 milliroentgens per hour by June 1970, and by 1971 the levels were not to exceed .5 milliroentgens even if the components controlling these circuits broke down. Apparently these are realistic criteria since the manufacturing establishment was adequately represented on the committee. It still leaves the possibility that many sets now in use could be a source of danger.

While the committee was wrestling with the problem of radiation in color television sets, it also tried to set standards for an appliance that is a more powerful source of radiation in the home. This appliance is the microwave oven. The microwave oven heats food rapidly using a source that is extremely high in dangerous radiation energy. The oven is built with adequate shielding or insulation to contain the radiation produced within it, but there is a possibility of leakage around the doors. Problems can arise from the failure of the oven to shut down as soon as the door is opened. The mechanism involved in shutting off the emission of radiation when the door is opened is called the interlock. A delay of even two seconds before the interlock actuates the cutoff of power can cause the operator to receive an unhealthy dose of radiation.

The fact that more and more of these ovens are being sold to American consumers points up the urgent need to set standards for their safe operation. It is chilling to realize that this appliance has been offered for sale to the public for over ten years without anyone's seriously inquiring about its safety.

The Tappan Company was the first to market this type of oven, in a range that sold for over $1200. Tappan was followed by Hotpoint and other companies, who incorporated the Tappan microwave oven into their own products. Now the ovens are being marketed mainly as a small accessory oven, not part of a full-size range. It has been selling well for the Amana division of the Raytheon Corporation for about $500. Other manufacturers are pushing plans to market their own brands of microwave ovens, and RCA has announced technological breakthroughs in the power supply that may bring a reduction in cost.

Whatever RCA has discovered, the Japanese must have already learned. Toshiba, Hitachi, and Matsushita are selling microwave ovens in quantity at home and threaten soon to invade the United States market with ovens priced substantially under $400. As the price of microwave ovens decreases and their distribution expands, it is imperative that the public be guaranteed their safe operation. This fact is underlined by recent tests in New York City that showed that seven out of eleven microwave ovens had radiation leakage. Similar tests in Florida showed leakage in 40 percent of commercial ovens and up to 25 percent of those in home use.

Until the blowup of the radiation peril in the national press, no one in industry or government was terribly concerned about the safety of home appliances. Except for *Consumer Reports'* continuous crusade against appliances with electric shock hazards, little attention was paid to the dangers to life and property that these appliances could present.

The industry was content to leave the inspection of their products to Underwriters Laboratories, and once the appliance has received the UL label it is home free. Situations in which high-temperature-limiting switches fail in dryers, causing them to overheat and burn up, cannot be checked out 100 percent by UL.

Inherently unsafe design permitted lint to accumulate in an inaccessible space between the inner and outer drums of some clothes dryers. Some of this lint eventually came in contact with heating coils and ignited. Dishwashers are designed with insufficient spacing between the heating coil and the racks. No warning was given to the housewife that a plastic utensil either placed or falling on the bottom rack was apt to go up in flames.

Portable television sets had extremely haphazard shock protection—until some years ago, when a small boy in Ohio touched a General Electric set near his family's pool and was electrocuted. This accident was caused by electrical current leakage to the metal cabinet. The youngster, probably with wet bare feet, touched the metal cabinet, and his body acted as a perfect ground. The danger was reduced when sets using circuits prone to this type of hazard were required to use a polarized plug at the end of the line cord. Television sets now have one broad and one narrow prong on their plugs. With this configuration they will only fit into the wall receptacle one way and are thus properly grounded.

One group of appliance manufacturers who have been historically alert to the dangers inherent in their products has been the Gas Appliances Manufacturers Association. This organization requires its members to submit any new product or device using gas to a testing laboratory maintained by the association. In order to earn the association's seal of approval, the product must conform to a reasonable standard of safety and reliability. The consumer buying a gas appliance should look for the GAMA seal, which is usually displayed on or near the plate bearing the model and serial number. This seal provides an assurance that the product has been screened by a group committed to safeguarding the reputation of gas as a fuel and the appliances that are made for its use.

This is an example of a segment of the appliance industry banding together for the purpose of self-policing and promotion. Rather than risk the unfavorable publicity which could result from an epidemic of accidents involving gas appliances, the association's members see to it that one manufacturer's inferior product doesn't ruin the image of the whole gas industry. It is only recently and in response to the Presidential Task Force on Major Appliance Warranties and Service that the Association of Home Appliance Manufacturers (AHAM) has made a start in the direction of applying uniform standards. Committees are being set up within that organization to deal more effectively with consumer complaints, eliminate deceptive advertising, and establish a consumer information bureau. The request by the government that they set up a system similar to the automobile industry's of notification and recall of appliances found to be unsafe is still under study.

The appliance industry knows it has to become more consumer-oriented in its approach to problems of safety, durability, and service. Accelerating the industry's efforts have been the passage of legislation by a Congress suddenly sympathetic to the cause of the consumer and the threat of even more onerous governmental controls. By cleaning up their own backyard, the appliance makers hope to avoid the embarrassing publicity and the expensive and burdensome legislation which the inertia of automobile manufacturers brought upon themselves.

So far, legislation affecting the appliance industry has been of a tentative or fact-finding nature. In November 1967, the 90th Congress created the National Commission on Product Safety. Its mission, as stated in a fact sheet it supplied, is:

to develop effective means to protect the American consumer from unreasonable hazards in many products commonly used in and around the home today. It was established after Congressional inquiry showed that hundreds of thousands of Americans each year are injured—or even killed—by such products.

One of the Commission's jobs is to identify the products that endanger health or safety. The Commission also intends to take steps to correct the hazards it uncovers.

After reviewing and evaluating existing Federal, State and local laws and industry's self-regulatory programs intended to protect the consumer, the Commission will propose measures to assure more effective protection for the future.

The commission so far has held hearings in several major American cities and has taken testimony regarding the danger of death or injury from children's toys, power mowers, home appliances, and tools. At the Boston hearings on December 19, 1968, the commission chairman, Arnold B. Elkind, expressed his disappointment in the failure of the news media to report completely the proceedings of the commission. Elkind pointed out that although brand names of hazardous products were mentioned at the Boston hearings, neither the press nor television in Boston used the manufacturers' names. Chairman Elkind declared that he believed the press should make public the names of unreasonably hazardous products in order to guide the consumer.

As a result of the commission's findings, legislation has been proposed calling for the elimination of the possibility of death by entrapment in refrigeration equipment. This would call for an amendment to existing federal law assuring that freezer doors meet the same requirements as refrigerators. This means that they are made to be opened from the inside without the use of a mechanical latch and with a minimum of outward pressure.

After several hearings UL agreed to advance from December 1, 1969, the date by which all UL-listed refrigerators and freezers had to be grounded. Also, UL amended its requirements for electric hair curlers to include a back-up safety device to prevent fire or shock in the case of thermostat failure. Underwriters Laboratories decided that the cords attached to electrical appliances will no longer be labeled "UL" unless the total appliance meets UL standards and test requirements. An important concession by UL was the increasing of consumer representation in the process involved in setting standards.

In his appearance before the National Commission on Product Safety on February 19, 1969, Baron Whitaker, the president of UL, made an effective presentation of the history, methods, and objectives of Underwriters Laboratories. In essence, UL is a nonprofit corporation whose purpose is "to help get safe equipment into the hands of the public." Its operations are unique in that this private organization develops standards, operates testing laboratories and follows up its findings at the factory level to see that its standards are being adhered to in production. It also provides the distinctive UL label, by which approved products can be identified by the public.

UL fears that further governmental penetration into the area of product safety may bring a call for federal testing laboratories. This is a step that could make the function of UL redundant. In order to forestall that eventuality, Whitaker proposed a program to the commission that would create joint industry and governmental groups to collect and analyze information regarding accidents associated with the use of household appliances. They would also provide for the dissemination of this information to manufacturers, installers, and code writers so that remedial action could be taken. They would set up a governmental group of technical experts who would check compliance with safety standards and work with UL in developing new standards.

For its own part, UL plans to embark on an advertising program designed to make the public familiar with what UL is and with how to benefit from its findings. As for its testing programs, industry can expect a tightening of UL's control over compliance and an upgrading of its standards as they affect hazards to individuals.

This is a departure from its past concern mainly with fire and electrical hazards.

The government hopes to accomplish its goal of improving the safety of products used by the American consumer by relying on private industry to regulate itself. However, the threat of federal regulation is very real to the manufacturers if they fail now to grasp this last opportunity to take full responsibility for the goods they produce.

12

Yes, Virginia,
There Is a Problem

CAN THE CONSUMER expect that his position will be improved the next time he buys an appliance or television set? Up to the present the retail buyer has been the victim of sharp selling practices, goods that failed to perform, and warranties that sought to disavow responsibility rather than to protect. Service has ranged from good to indifferent to bad.

One can detect hopeful signs that help is on the way. Since the plight of the consumer has been made a hot political issue, more concrete legislation has been enacted or is contemplated to safeguard the buyer's interests. The federal Truth-in-lending law now demands that the buyer be made aware of exactly what his borrowing costs will be and the true rate of interest that he will pay. It does not yet set any reasonable limit on how much that rate should be. That has been left to the legislatures of the various states. Lack of uniformity in these state codes results in the unrealistically low rate of 8 percent in some states to the almost usurious 18 percent and higher in others. But the federal law does prevent the use in advertising of credit terms such as "Only $2.25 a week," as a sales gimmick. Anyone advertising a specific dollar amount payment must also advertise the full price of the article, the down payment required, and the total price including finance charges. That should pretty well discourage the misleading advertising of credit terms.

The establishment of the National Commission on Product Safety in 1967 and the 1968 Federal Radiation Standards law reflects the congressional concern for the safety of the products sold to the American public. These agencies, even if they do not produce significant legislative reforms, have had a salutary effect for the consumer. They have unearthed abuses, discovered potentially dangerous products, and have exposed the products and their makers to the glare of publicity. They are a warning to industry that the government is ready to regulate its operations severely if industry fails to improve its responsiveness to the needs and rights of the consumer.

The report of the Presidential Task Force on Major Appliance Warranties and Service has prodded the appliance industry to begin constructive programs designed to make available to the consumer some redress for his complaints. There is still a gap between what the government would like the industry to do and how far the appliance manufacturers are willing to go.

The best long-range hope for all consumers, and particularly the appliance buyer, lies in the office of the Presidential Adviser for Consumer Affairs. This bureau and its chief act purely in an advisory capacity and lack executive power. However, under the aggressive leadership of Betty Furness and the promising activity of Mrs. Virginia Knauer the agency could prove of great benefit to the consumer. Mrs. Knauer is especially interested in the appliance industry as it affects the consumer. She is crusading for the availability of more complete information to the buyer in regard to warranties, access to service and parts, and even in relative operating costs between models and brands.

Operating under a curtailed budget and an administration whose domestic program lacks any real consumer orientation, Mrs. Knauer has to rely on persuasion and publicity to achieve her aims. Her ultimate weapon is the recommendation to Congress of legislation to correct abuses she uncovers in the market place. An example of this type of lawmaking is a bill being prepared which would permit consumers to bring suit as a class or group against a manufacturer or merchant engaging in unfair or deceptive trade practices.

This law would make it possible for a group of consumers to recover losses by sharing the legal costs, which would probably be so high as to discourage an individual from bringing an action in federal court. Ralph Nader, the consumers' watch dog, says that this bill falls far short of what is needed to protect the consumer and that it is merely a gesture by the administration rather than a real reform.

Along other lines, Mrs. Knauer's office is called upon to testify on a wide range of consumer bills in addition to working for the establishment of consumer-protection agencies in all fifty states operating under uniform codes.

The appliance industry's concern over governmental regulation is reflected in a speech by James T. McMurphy, director of distribution for the Philco-Ford Corporation. His remarks to a group of appliance dealers at a NARDA seminar in Washington, D.C., were reported in the August 8, 1969, edition of *Home Furnishings Daily:*

The first step in stamping out consumerism is to return the customer to his former lofty position of king. If customers really believed they were king and queen of the appliance business I think they would be boosters of ours rather than detractors or anti-customers. . . . Why wait for a power grab or a seized opportunity by some public or private agency? . . . There must be a determination within the industry to identify and fix problems without the necessity of outside prodding or regulations.

Industry is obviously worried about the encroachment of regulatory controls into what was once, for them, a laissez-faire business. Appliance manufacturers, through their trade associations like AHAM and GAMA, are working to standardize and simplify product warranties. How much responsibility for the effective implementation of these warranties they will take upon themselves remains to be seen. What is needed is assurance that a consumer not receiving adequate service or satisfaction at a local level can go to a factory and get prompt action and not buck-passing correspondence.

An attempt at this kind of national clearinghouse for the consumer complaints has been instituted by the Whirlpool Corporation. They have made available to the public a toll-free telephone number through which a consumer in any part of the country can call and receive advice or service on a piece of Whirlpool equipment. Sears, Roebuck has advertised a similar setup by which Sears' customers can get service regardless of what part of the country the appliance was purchased. If these super service agencies can actually perform as advertised, it would behoove the other appliance manufacturers to move quickly into this area.

The appliance manufacturers, including Whirlpool,

must depend on both their factory-controlled service operations and independent dealers and service contractors. The manufacturers recognize that factory-controlled service companies would provide the best and most uniform service of their products. General Electric, Frigidaire, Westinghouse, and Philco-Ford are speeding up the take-over of the service function in most of the larger markets. In more rural areas, the sheer size of the geographical spaces that must be covered make this type of factory-owned agency economically unfeasible. When factories must depend on outside servicing facilities, they should make it their prime concern that the servicemen not under their direct control are technically competent. Attendance at factory-operated training sessions should be made compulsory and not at the whim or convenience of the service people. In order to qualify as authorized service agents these men should be required to pass periodic examinations, which would assure their proficiency in repairing the appliances for which they are responsible. Upgrading the quality of servicemen would tend to minimize the frustration generated by servicemen who, when they finally do arrive, cannot pinpoint the difficulty or do an incompetent job, causing frequent callbacks.

While everyone agrees that there is a shortage of servicemen, not enough is being done to recruit and train new ones. Factories should encourage and assist vocational and technical high schools to install training programs aimed at turning out well-grounded potential appliance servicemen. For a young man not seeking a college education it is a well-paying trade with a relatively short apprenticeship.

Although electronic equipment is being made more

and more sophisticated and no great increase in the supply of highly trained technicians is anticipated, the outlook from the standpoint of service is bright. Here, the state of the art has advanced so rapidly that the incorporation of solid-state devices and miniature and microminiature circuits and modules has reduced the incidence of failure dramatically. Complete circuits the size of a pinhead are capable of performing all of the functions of an ordinary radio. Motorola's pioneering design of a completely modular solid-state color television set permits circuits to be plugged into a chassis affording quick repair by less highly skilled technicians. RCA also makes an all-solid-state color television set, and Zenith and other manufacturers are using one or more solid-state modular circuits in their sets. While most of these circuits are still wired together, it will not be long before the Motorola concept of a television set whose circuits can be taken apart and put together like a Tinker Toy will be universally adopted.

The impact that improved reliability and ease of service will have on the electronics service industry has already been recognized. At a recent convention of TV and electronics servicemen, a spokesman indicated that his colleagues would soon find it necessary to increase their labor charges. With less incidence of breakdown, and with the manufacturer guaranteeing replacement of solid-state components for up to five years, the serviceman can look forward to sharply curtailed income from replacement parts.

With the cost of electronics servicing bound to rise, the consumer may find at the expiration of the warranty period that it is more expedient to replace a radio, portable phonograph, or television set than to have it repaired, for while advanced technology has improved the performance, reliability, and life expectancy of electronic products, it has also accelerated their obsolescence by making them a disposable commodity.

Appliance manufacturers are quick to point out that their products offer better value to the consumer than almost anything else he buys. It is true that appliance and television set prices have risen far less than the average of other commodities, and that more capacity and convenience features have been built into them. This has been accomplished by the employment of substitute materials, more modern production facilities, and an expanding market capable of absorbing the increased output of these more efficient plants.

The appliance industry's service problems arise from the fact that although most manufacturers have increased the square footage of their factories and are pushing for all the production they can get, they have not been able to supply the demand. For most of 1968 and 1969, deliveries of major appliances to distributors and dealers lagged far behind orders. In the third quarter of 1968, Westinghouse was able to fill only 25 percent of its orders for electric ranges. A long strike at the Tecumseh Company, which produces compressors for refrigerators and air conditioners, seriously hamstrung production of those items for a number of companies.

With the dealers' pressure for more goods outrunning the ability to supply, it was natural that quality control and inspection would suffer. This is the situation that gives rise to the dealers' sad stories of refrigerators that are dead on arrival or air conditioners with refrigerant leaks or television sets that must be run in the store for twenty-four hours before the dealers dare to deliver them. If one adds an occasional instance of industrial sabotage at the factory, the situation can become chaotic.

Westinghouse was the victim of this intentional carelessness at its Columbus, Ohio, refrigeration plant in 1967. The labor unions had a list of grievances that were not being resolved. Since they were still working under a contract they could not strike, but they expressed their dissatisfaction by taking it out on the product. For a period of about three months, refrigerators were shipped with sloppy-fitting trim parts, extra screws rattling around, and finish blemishes that were caught by the inspectors but left uncorrected. Westinghouse quietly admitted that it was aware of these conditions but asked that the dealers bear with the company. When the labor problems at the factory were settled, quality improved to a level equal to any other manufacturer's.

The appliance makers fight to remain at competitive pricing levels by driving their factories for increased output and their distributors and dealers for greater market penetration. In this constant cost-cutting battle they are hampered by the large number of models, features, and colors they feel they must offer. Refrigerators are made with right- or left-hand doors, with or without ice makers, and in as many as ten different sizes. In each of the sizes, models are offered with fewer or more features in order to have several price stepups within a single cubic-foot-size range. In addition, practically every model is offered in a choice of white, coppertone, avocado, or gold.

The same proliferation of models exists in washers, dryers, and ranges. Adding an extra knob or push button makes for an extra model in the line, and again it has to be made in four delicious flavors. General Electric makes a refrigerator that can spit out ice cubes or ice water through a gadget on the outside of the cabinet. Frigidaire offers an electric range that dispenses hot water from a faucet on its control panel. Are these extra-cost items really what the consumer needs or is asking for, or are they merely put into the line as image builders and conversation pieces?

The mere addition of mechanical refinements does not ensure a better or more reliable product. An owner of a new, top-of-the-line General Electric Versatronic automatic washing machine had this story to tell. About four weeks after installation the machine broke down. A serviceman from the General Electric factory service branch came to her house, looked at the washer, and said he would have to order a part. Three weeks later the serviceman showed up with what proved to be the wrong part. After another week of daily acrimonious telephone calls to the service branch, a new washer of the same model was delivered. It was not installed by General Electric, nor was the first machine removed. The husband had to hook up the replacement washer, and after two days that one failed in the same manner as the first: it would not go into the spin cycle.

A General Electric serviceman showed up the next day, looked at the washer, and said he couldn't fix it but would send out another man. The second serviceman came out later that afternoon and repaired the second machine and said, "We've been having a lot of trouble with these Versatronics. They haven't got all the bugs out yet." The first machine is still in the customer's garage.

The appliance and electronics manufacturers could go

far toward controlling the inevitable upward spiraling of their costs and selling prices by abandoning the expensive restyling and retooling they go through when they give birth to new models. Very little in the nature of a major technical breakthrough occurs between one model of a refrigerator, washer, TV, or stereo and the next year's model. Most of the distinction has to come from purely design or styling modifications. Any real mechanical improvements should be incorporated into current production and not held back to be introduced in next year's models.

Magnavox has been successful without ever identifying any television set or stereo with a model year. New models are introduced throughout the course of the year and others are dropped. The discontinued numbers never become stigmatized as "last year's models," and the dealers a fresh batch of warmed-over models every year, the long as the manufacturers continue to dump on the dealers a fresh batch of warmed-up models every year, the consumer has a right to know if they are current or not. This is one of the items on Mrs. Knauer's list of things that should be fully disclosed to the consumer.

No real benefit accrues to the buyer by a change of model number simply because the calendar says it is due. A greater benefit might be derived by the refining of a product to the point where its reliability is enhanced and its price brought down by amortizing the tooling costs over a longer period of time.

Home Furnishings Daily reported these comments by Jay Doblin, director of the Institute of Design, Illinois Institute of Technology, made at the annual meeting of the Association of Home Appliance Manufacturers in May 1969:

Instead of dreaming up new appliance innovations, manufacturers should begin to think about denovating them.

Manufacturers will be forced to denovate appliances because consumers will soon become wise and not want to spend extra dollars for fancy trimmings suppliers call design. . . . People will soon realize they don't need extra features and will want products with less chrome, leather and any other costly additions.

Doblin also gave the symptoms and diseases with which he feels the appliance and home electronics industries are suffering:

Accumulosis—an accumulation of needless materials on any given appliance.

Symbago—an ordinary appliance which is introduced every year with more and more extras.

Eyeorrhoea—a social disease. This makes most appliances look like a brand-new Buick.

The appliance manufacturers seem to feel that it is in distribution rather than production that future important economies can be achieved. General Electric has announced plans for a new manufacturing and distribution complex outside of Baltimore that eventually could equal its huge Appliance Park facilities in Louisville, Kentucky. Frigidaire and Whirlpool have built major distribution centers in Harrisburg, Pennsylvania, and Columbus, Ohio. The purpose of these superwarehouses is to phase out the maintenance of a large number of smaller depots all over the country. This would save a lot of payroll at these branches, and the big depots could be expected to stock a wider assortment of models in greater depth.

The route to survival recommended to the independent appliance dealer is the formation of cooperatives. One kind of cooperative buying group could be similar to MARTA, in which dealers pool their purchasing for the purpose of earning the lowest possible prices. Another is the pooling of dealers' inventories. By maintaining only floor samples and sharing warehouse backup stocks with dealers carrying the same lines, a dealer can greatly reduce the amount of capital needed to finance his business.

The successful large-volume independent appliance dealer has still another recourse: he can sell out at a profit, a route taken recently by Certified TV and Appliance of Norfolk, Virginia. This three-store chain was acquired by Wards Company, a publicly held corporation headquartered in Richmond. Wards operates dozens of appliance and television stores either under its own name or as leased departments in major discount stores from coast to coast. The president of Certified TV is Ezra Landres, a vice-president of NARDA, who has been a vocal champion for the independent appliance dealer. Landres commented upon his acquisition by Wards Company in *Mart*, an appliance-trade publication:

The days of the independent retailer . . . are fast coming to a close. Distribution has reached a point where we simply cannot compete with the buying power of the mass merchandisers. Customers are willing to sacrifice the attention and service provided by the independent, but not by the chains, for price alone. Independents must join with others in order to survive.

What can the consumer do to ensure his survival when he ventures into the appliance market? The political climate has changed in favor of the retail buyer, and congressional sentiment seems to be finally on his side. Hopefully, present or threatened legislation and watchdog agencies will stir the industry into long overdue reform.

But it is up to the individual, lonely shopper to arm himself with all the knowledge he can gather before he makes his next appliance purchase. He can do some very productive research in the back issues of *Consumer Reports* at his public library. While he does not have to follow that magazine's buying recommendations slavishly, it will provide a lot of information on the product he is interested in. Points of construction, operating cost, convenience, and safety that most laymen are not aware of will be discussed.

When the buyer has determined what brand and model is best suited to his needs and budget, he should shop to find it at the price, terms, and delivery time most favorable to him. Any promises concerning warranties and service responsibility should be secured in writing. If after the purchase the product does not perform, the consumer should not be afraid to complain—first, to the dealer, next, to the factory (preferably by telegram), and, finally, to any consumer-protection group or even to his congressman.

It is only when the consumer knows what he wants and is vocal in demanding it that *caveat emptor* will truly be dead.

Index

189

National Video, 94-95
Ninety-day parts warranty, 92-93
Ninety-day purchase terms, 121
Norge appliances, 54, 55, 126, 138, 152

Obsolescence, 63-67, 179
Olympic appliances, 137-38
Overcharge system, 81

Penny, J. C. Company, 86, 149, 154
Philco-Bendix Division, 62
   washer-dryer combination, 23
Philco Corporation
   profits, 137
   refrigerators, 22
   TV servicing, 44, 95
Philco-Ford, 54, 55, 57, 104, 175, 177
Picture tubes, TV, warranties on, 92-96
Plastics, use of, 55-58
Prebilled-service method, 32, 36, 44
Presidential Task Force on Major Appliance Warranties and Service, 166, 174
Prices (pricing), 117-28, 131-40, 173-74, 179
   See also Profits; specific appliances, companies
Printed circuitry, 24-26, 60, 63
Profit-sharing program, Sears', 148
Profits, 54-67, 101-14, 131-40
   See also Prices (pricing)

"Qualifying the customer," 12-13

Radiation hazards, 159-65
Radio sets, 24-28, 56
Rauland picture tubes, 95
Raytheon Corporation, 164
RCA
   distribution, 104, 105
   microwave ovens, 164
   prices and profits, 55, 118-19, 132, 137
   radios, 25

service, 42-43, 94-95
television sets, 17-18, 26, 178
warranties, 94-95
RCA Victor, 63
Redisco, 126
Refrigerators
   buying, 11-13, 79, 133-35
   design and engineering, 17-21, 55-56, 57-59, 64-65, 66-67
   prices and profits, 53, 55, 57-59, 133-35
   sales techniques, 11-13, 79, 133-35
   servicing, 36, 66, 90-92, 179-80
   warranties, 90-92
Repairs, see Service; Warranties; specific appliances
Replacement parts, 47-49
Revolving credit plans, 122
Robinson-Patman Act, 107
Roper Company, 144

S. & H. Green Stamps, 73, 78
Safety hazards, 159-70, 174
Sales (sales techniques; salesmen), 12-13, 71-82, 99-114, 131-40, 145-48
Sales training programs, 147
Sales contracts, 121, 125-26
Sears, Roebuck & Co., 23, 35, 41, 86, 137, 139, 143-56
Service (servicing), 13, 27-28, 31-49, 176-78
   agencies (organizations), 13, 31-49
   second-year policies, 137, 138-39
   servicemen, 38, 177-78
   warranties, 85-96; See also Warranties; specific appliances
Service bulletins, 28
Service-dealers, 36, 45-46
Shopping (buying), 9-14, 117-28, 131-40, 173-85
Silvertone (Sears) brand, 41, 145, 151
Solid-state appliances, 26-28, 60, 65, 66, 178
"Spiffs," 72, 78, 108
Stereo sets, 56, 58, 92, 93, 120
Stromberg Carlson appliances, 12

Th........ ....ing this material